D0699373

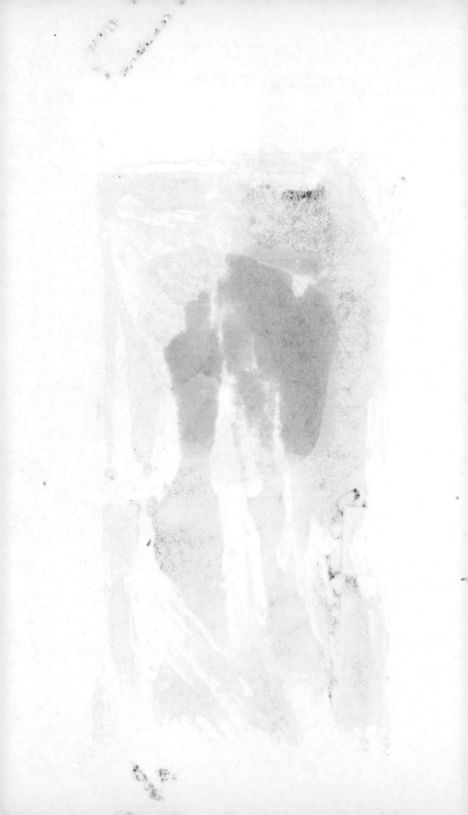

An Introduction to Greek Ethics

Christopher Rowe

Christopher Rowe was educated at Christ's Hospital
and at Trinity College, Cambridge, and has been
lecturer in Classics in the University of Bristol since
1968. He was a Visiting Fellow at the Institute for
Advanced Studies in the Humanities, University of
Edinburgh, in 1972, and a Junior Fellow at the
Center for Hellenic Studies, Washington, D.C., for
1974–5. His publications include a specialist
monograph on Aristotle's *Eudemian* and *Nicomachean
Ethics*.

Philosophy editor
Professor S. Körner
jur.Dr., Ph.D., F.B.A.
Professor of Philosophy
University of Bristol
and Yale University

An Introduction to Greek Ethics

Christopher Rowe

Lecturer in Classics,
University of Bristol

BOOKS
10 East 53d St., New York 10022
(a division of Harper & Row Publishers, Inc.)

First published 1976 by
Hutchinson & Co (Publishers) Ltd, London

Published in the USA 1977 by
Harper & Row Publishers Inc.
Barnes & Noble Import Division

Printed in Great Britain
ISBN 0 06 496008 0

BJ 182
. R87

Contents

Acknowledgements

A large part of this book was written during 1974–75 in the pleasant surroundings of the Center for Hellenic Studies, Washington, D.C. I am grateful to several colleagues and friends at the Center for help of various kinds; but especially to the Director, Professor Bernard Knox, without whom the Center could not be the place that it is. I should also like to thank Professor David Furley, of Princeton University, who made detailed and helpful criticisms of Chapters 3 and 4; an anonymous American reader; my wife Heather, for advice, and for help with typing; and finally Professor Stephan Körner, for much kindly encouragement.

Note on Transliteration

Greek words appear in the text in transliterated form. The Roman letter, or pair of letters, used to represent each Greek letter is the one which corresponds most closely to it in the (largely incorrect) pronunciation employed by most British scholars. Vowels are short unless marked long; $\bar{e}$ is pronounced not as in 'me' but rather as the 'ê' in the French 'bête'.

Where Greek words are included, this is for one of two reasons: either because they are key terms, for which there may be no precise equivalents in English (these are, of course, always explained as far as necessary in the appropriate contexts); or, more occasionally, where the translation of a particular term or expression might be open to question, to indicate to the reader with Greek, the word or words in the original which are being rendered.

Introduction

'The function of moral philosophy', says R. M. Hare in the preface to *Freedom and Reason*, ' . . . is that of helping us to think better about moral questions by exposing the logical structure of the language in which this thought is expressed.' This statement gives a fair characterization of the general preoccupation of British and American moral philosophers over the last half-century. The Greek philosophers thought differently. For them, the aims of moral philosophy were at all times essentially practical in nature. Its chief concern was not with the theoretical analysis of the nature of moral discourse, but with the establishment and justification of particular systems of conduct. Even Aristotle, otherwise the most theoretical of all the Greek ethical philosophers, says quite firmly that the final aim of his inquiry is not just to know what goodness is, but to become good. Although a great deal of his work is concerned with analysis and elucidation of moral terms, his ultimate goal is always a prescriptive one; description serves only as a preliminary to prescription.

The starting-point of Greek moral philosophy, from the fifth-century sophists until the Hellenistic period, is the question about how a man is to live his life: what is the final human good? What constitutes happiness, *eudaimoniā*? So Plato asks us to choose between a life of justice and a life of injustice, while Aristotle begins by weighing up the claims of the lives of pleasure, honour, and scientific contemplation. Both attempt to show that goodness is crucial to happiness; and Socrates, too, agrees. Others saw happiness as consisting in the possession of wealth and power, or in the pursuit of short-term pleasures.

It might be objected that a general inquiry into the nature of human happiness is doomed from the start; what makes a man happy is, we might say, having what he most desires, but his desires may be entirely peculiar to him. The point was effectively recognized by Aristotle, who simply replied that it is the good man's desires which must serve as the criterion. Given the best possible individual, we can say that happiness will consist in virtuous activity. In much the same vein, Socrates and Plato introduce the notion of mental health: if we were in our right minds, we would desire virtue, the only true good. Stated in this crude form, the arguments are hopelessly circular; but they are parts of a serious attempt to deal with a crucial problem, the problem of providing a reasoned justification for moral beliefs. This problem will be one of the main themes of this book. A second will be the connected problem of the nature and source of moral knowledge. If acting rightly is a part of happiness, then the analysis of happiness must include an account of the criteria to be employed in the moral decisions on which it depends. Around this second problem arose one of the most interesting disputes in Greek philosophy.

A variety of answers was given; yet none is of a kind which might be of any real help in resolving particular issues of conduct. What begins as a specifically practical exercise ends by providing us with sets of formal principles which seem to get us little further than the position from which we started, that we should live a life of virtue. Aristotle, and to a lesser extent Plato, do go on to attempt a more precise picture of the virtuous life. But the sketches are two-dimensional, and betray little awareness of the difficult and complex nature of real situations. It is certainly true that Aristotle elsewhere explicitly recognizes at least part of that complexity, and moreover makes it into a central feature of his analysis of the problem of moral knowledge. Individuals differ, and situations differ; hence, he concludes, it must be impossible to give answers which apply equally in all cases. But this point in itself effectively prevents him from giving any but the most general recommendations about conduct. Particular decisions in particular situations must be left to the individual agent, and right decisions will flow from right dispositions.

This looks a reasonable position, so far as it goes. But it means that the practical contribution which the philosopher can make is severely circumscribed. By contrast, Hare's initially more restricted approach issues in a principle for which he claims 'great potency in moral arguments, – and one which, if right, would also provide help in just those situations where we most need it, situations where even the most well-meaning people find themselves in fundamental disagreement. Aristotle's criterion, which depends on a consensus of responsible opinion, necessarily fails to cover such cases, although elsewhere he certainly recognizes their existence; one example is his long discussion in the first book of the *Politics* of the rights and wrongs of slavery, which is in many ways (despite its very different conclusions) directly comparable with Hare's discussion of racial conflicts in the final chapter of *Freedom and Reason.*

Thus my initial distinction between the practical concerns of the Greek philosophers and the theoretical concerns of their modern counterparts clearly requires some qualification; but it is nonetheless real and important. In spite of the generality of its conclusions, Greek ethics is predominantly moralistic in tone. Its primary aim is not to help to clear our minds, but to inculcate a set of values. The dialogues of Plato suggest that the moral climate of contemporary Greece was one of extreme uncertainty. The atmosphere of crisis is to some extent exaggerated; but certainly much of the literature of the time does provide evidence of a new readiness to question and criticize the assumptions of contemporary morality. For all their dissatisfaction with conventional attitudes, Socrates and Plato can plausibly be regarded as representatives of the intellectual conservative reaction. The sophists had argued that traditional morality rested on convention, *nomos.* Some, like Protagoras, insisted that it was a useful convention, which must be preserved; without it, society would collapse. Others saw it merely as a device used by the weak to protect themselves against the strong, and proposed to substitute a Machiavellian theory of natural justice. Nevertheless, both parties shared the same view of traditional justice, as a compact founded on need. Socrates and Plato responded by attempting to restore it to its place in nature: the just was not just because it was beneficial to society, or to a particular group in society, but it was beneficial because it was just. Benefits would flow from justice, both for society and for the individual, but it was not determined by those benefits. They saw this not as an academic dispute, but as one of enormous and immediate practical relevance.

Aristotle's approach is more detached. But there is no doubt that he belongs firmly within the Socratic-Platonic tradition. What characterized that tradition more than anything was the conviction that moral disagreement only occurs because of a lack of knowledge; simple answers exist, if only we knew how to find them (an ideal, unsurprisingly, never realized). Aristotle replies – though, as we will see, much the same point is made in a late dialogue by Plato himself – that this is to misunderstand the nature of the subject-matter of ethics, which does not allow the precision achievable in the theoretical sciences. But he still thinks that all mature and adult people will roughly agree about the answer to any given problem; it will always be possible to say what sort of thing ought to be done, even if it is not possible to specify it exactly. Thus he too finally rejects the relativist view of morality canvassed by the sophists, in favour of a position not so very different from that of Socrates and Plato.

It is the three figures of Socrates, Plato and Aristotle which will inevitably bulk largest in this book. There are two main reasons for this: firstly, they are the most interesting; and secondly, our evidence both for the period before Socrates and for the period after Aristotle is at best fragmentary. Our evidence about the Presocratic philosophers and the sophists, and about all the many post-Aristotelian schools, has to be pieced together painstakingly from a mass of often obscure and often conflicting reports by other writers. Interpretation is always difficult, and critical assessment doubly so. Yet what evidence we do have suggests that while they have much of value to offer in other fields, both periods are of essentially secondary interest for moral philosophy.

The reasons are different in the two cases. The importance of the sophists is mainly historical; while they were responsible, directly or indirectly, for raising some of the central questions which preoccupied later philosophers, their own concern with ethical philosophy was, in general, no more than incidental. Protagoras and Gorgias, probably the two most influential of the sophists, were teachers of rhetoric, and their excursions into ethical theory, such as they were, were essentially the result of their professional interest in language as a means of persuasion. Other early figures, like Heraclitus and Democritus, are largely content to repeat the truths of traditional wisdom, although there are traces in both of interesting attempts to provide a bridge between moral and physical principles. The post-Aristotelian schools, on the other hand, were limited rather by their narrowness and dogmatism. The Socratic ideal of philosophy as an inquiry after truth is for the most part absent from the moral philosophy of the Hellenistic period; and the result is a series of closed systems which are more remarkable for their economy and consistency than for their philosophical insight. (Others give a rather higher evaluation: see especially the recent book on *Hellenistic Philosophy* by A. A. Long.)

This verdict is harsh, but fair. The Hellenistic philosophies were, more than anything, a response to an emotional need. Both Plato and Aristotle had regarded ethics as part of the science of politics, whose function it was to provide the conditions under which the individual members of the community could achieve happiness. This attitude reflected the importance in contemporary Greek politics of the small, autonomous city-state, or *polis*. Aristotle himself saw the *polis* as the natural end-point of political development. But with the coming of Alexander such a restricted viewpoint could no longer be sustained. For the first time, the Greeks were forced to come to terms with a wider environment, beyond the limits both of the city-state and of the Greek world. Reaction took two forms, both of which are to be found in Stoicism. One is positive, one negative: on the one hand, the Stoics put forward a doctrine of the universal brotherhood of man, which contrasts sharply with the unbendingly chauvinistic attitudes of earlier periods; and on the other, they promote the negative ideal of *apatheia,* freedom from violent feeling and emotion, which is to guarantee invulnerability against a hostile world. This second reaction is the more typical of the Hellenistic philosophers as a whole. The need is for security; and it is this need which shapes their systems.

Of course, Socrates and Plato were themselves responding to a particular historical situation; but they did so in a fundamentally reasoned way. Although both began from passionate and deeply held convictions, it was for them a matter of the utmost importance that those convictions should be rationally based. Philosophy was a matter of debate, of 'two going together', as Plato puts it, quoting Homer. The same attitude is even more apparent in the dry, impersonal arguments of the Aristotelian treatises.

It is their reasonableness that constitutes the chief claim of Socrates, Plato, and Aristotle on our attention. But it is also clear that many of the problems with which they deal remain of crucial importance to moral philosophy, however its aims are understood. Of these, I identified the two most central: first, the problem of the justification of moral beliefs; and, second, the problem of moral knowledge. It is true that both initially arise in the context of a particular system of values, but in so far as they are treated in a philosophical way, the answers given to them necessarily acquire a more general applicability.

Linguistic and cultural differences must, of course, be taken into account. 'It is an elementary commonplace', says Alasdair MacIntyre, 'to point out that there is no precise English equivalent for the Greek word *dikaiosunē,* usually translated *justice.* And this is not a mere linguistic defect, so that what Greek achieves by a single word English needs a periphrasis to achieve. It is rather that the occurrence of certain concepts in ancient Greek discourse and of others in modern English marks a difference between two forms of social life. . . . So it would be a fatal mistake to write as if, in the history of moral philosophy, there had been one single task of analysing the concept of, for example, justice, to the performance of which Plato, Hobbes, and Bentham all set themselves, and for their achievement at which they can be awarded higher or lower marks' (*A Short History of Ethics,* pp. 1–2). MacIntyre sees it as one of the functions of the history of moral philosophy to provide 'an adequate historical view of the varieties of moral and evaluative discourse', as a corrective to those analytical philosophers who construct a suitably stable set of objects for moral philosophy by assuming the existence of a single universal language of morals. In the context of the particular dispute in which he is here involved, it is natural that he should lay the stress he does on the divergence between the moral concepts of different societies. But for my own present purposes such differences are less important. As MacIntyre himself admits, there is clearly sufficient overlap between the Greek concept of *dikaiosunē* and the English concept of justice to make what Plato or Aristotle says about the one directly relevant to what we may want to say about the other. Again, however great the differences between Greek and English moral usage, the nature of the larger problems – about the justification of moral principles, and about epistemology – remains unaffected. These are, perhaps, problems which arise from the very existence of moral terms in a language. (There is a very convenient account of the term *dikaiosunē*, in its classical use, in Aristotle's *Ethics*: see Ch. 7. One other central term deserves to be mentioned here, the term *eudaimoniā,* which I earlier rendered as 'happiness'. *Eudaimoniā* differs from 'happiness' in that it refers, not so much to a subjective feeling of contentment, as to other people's judgement about a man's condition. He is *eudaimōn* if he has the good things of life – whatever those may be; in ordinary language, *eudaimoniā* tends to be synonymous with material prosperity, while some of the philosophers, as I have said, equate it with the possession of a rather higher kind of good. But the subjective element will also normally be present, in so far as contentment seems a necessary part of the good life, however conceived [cf. Aristotle, *Ethics* 1095 b 31 *ff.*])

Thus, by and large, the arguments of Greek philosophy can be treated straightforwardly as contributions to a live and continuing debate. At the same time, however, it is as well to remember that if they are worth discussing at all, they are worth discussing as they are, not in some notional form that they might have had. It is all too easy to slip into talking about models of historical theories, based on our own ideas and assumptions, rather than the theories themselves; in which case, honesty and economy would suggest that the reference to a historical text should be dispensed with altogether. This book is written in the firm belief that the Greek philosophers deserve consideration in their own right.

One final point. There exists a large body of secondary literature on the subject matter treated in the following chapters; and many parts of it are the subject of controversy among scholars. I shall refer only rarely to this literature; although, of course, the views stated will have been partly formed by reading it. My aim is to provide a direct and continuous interpretation of the ancient material. Experience has convinced me that this is the best method of introduction; it provides at least some measure of solid ground, from which the reader can enter as he wishes into the tides of scholarly debate, but without which he might easily drown. (A selection of the secondary literature is given in the Bibliography.)

The structure of the book is largely self-explanatory. I begin with two brief chapters which are intended to sketch in something of the cultural and intellectual background against which Socrates and Plato worked: one on the development of Greek moral and religious views down to the fifth century; and one on the sophists. There then follows the main part, the treatment of Socrates, Plato and Aristotle. The three chapters on Plato and the chapter on Aristotle are designed as introductions to the main texts; full references are given. Finally there is a short chapter on the two main post-Aristotelian schools, the Epicureans and Stoics.

1 Justice and the gods: from Homer to the fifth century

I shall take as the starting-point of this chapter the climax of Homer's *Odyssey*, in which the returned Odysseus, with the help of his son Telemachus, slaughters the suitors of his faithful wife Penelope. It is perhaps natural for us to interpret this in terms of a triumph of good over evil. E. R. Dodds, in his important book *The Greeks and the Irrational,* describes it as a 'vindication of divine justice'. And there is much in the text of the poem to support this interpretation. Odysseus, addressing his old nurse Eurycleia, declares that it was 'the *moira* of the gods, the suitors' own cruelty (*schetlia erga*)' that tamed them. The line certainly smacks of divine retribution, of the idea that the gods punished the suitors for their wickedness: 'they maltreated anyone coming near them', Odysseus says, 'whatever his status – and that, and their recklessness, brought them to their end' (XXII 413–16). The phrase 'the *moira* of the gods' needs some explanation: *moira* is literally a man's 'share', or 'lot'; and each of us is given our *moira* by the gods (XIX 592–3). Sometimes *moira* is thought of as something independent of the gods, an impersonal 'fate'; sometimes it is personalized. But these rather different conceptions of *moira* are clearly not involved in the present context. Odysseus tells us, then, that the death of the suitors was appointed by the gods; and it seems reasonable to assume that it was appointed because of the suitors' behaviour. This is confirmed by a passage in the following book, where Penelope virtually repeats Odysseus' words, but actually says that 'one of the immortals killed the noble suitors, angry at their heart-grieving violence (*hubris*) and their evil deeds' (XXIII 63–4). (The point of Penelope's speech is that it was one of the gods, and not Odysseus at all, who killed the suitors; she does not yet believe that her husband is home.) And there are other passages, too, which bear out Dodds's interpretation. In Book XXIV, Laertes says: 'Father Zeus, so there are still gods on lofty Olympus, if in truth the suitors have paid for their reckless violence' (351–2); and in Book XX, Philoetius the cowherd tells us that 'they [the suitors] take no notice of Odysseus' son in his house, nor do they fear the vengeance of the gods; for they long to share among themselves the possessions of the long absent king' (214–16). In the same tone, in Book XXI, Penelope claims that the suitors' behaviour will bring them ill repute among the people (331 *ff.*). Finally, there is another speech by Odysseus himself, in Book XXII, in which he suggests to the suitors that they should have feared divine *nemesis* for eating his property, forcing their attentions on his maidservants, and wooing his wife while he was still alive (35 *ff.*).

One other passage is important in the present context. At the very beginning of the *Odyssey* (I 32 *ff.*), Zeus complains that humans blame the gods for the evil things that happen to them; 'but', he says, 'it is *they* who are responsible, through their own recklessness, if they have griefs beyond their share'. Aegisthus took Agamemnon's wife and killed him, knowing it would lead to his destruction; for Zeus claims that he told him that Orestes would avenge his father's death. But Aegisthus took no notice, and Orestes killed him. No doubt the same could be said of Aegisthus as of the suitors: 'he was tamed by the *moira* of the gods and his wickedness'. As Athena remarks, he deserved everything he got.

But the trouble with Dodds's view of the slaughter episode, as a vindication of divine justice, is that the suitors don't deserve what they get. Most of us, no doubt, would be inclined to feel that the suitors were guilty of *something*; but whatever their crime is, it scarcely seems great enough to warrant such violent retribution. That is to say, their treatment at the hands of Odysseus and Telemachus seems to have little to do with justice at all. One of the suitors, the priest Leodes, makes the justified claim that he tried to hold back the others; but he is slaughtered along with the rest, on the grounds that he must have hoped that Odysseus would never return. Melanthius the goatherd, who insulted Odysseus, has an especially nasty death: he has his nose, ears, genitals, hands and feet cut off. Revenge is what is uppermost in Odysseus' mind – revenge for personal injuries suffered at his enemies' hands.

The truth is, perhaps, that the moralizing tone belongs to Homer rather than to Odysseus. The code by which Homer's characters live – the code of Odysseus, no less than that of Aegisthus and the suitors – is the heroic one which plays so prominent a role in the *Iliad*; a code which dictates that personal glory and status are the only goals that matter. Homer's own attitudes are rather different. Charles Segal's conclusions about the *Iliad* seem equally applicable to the *Odyssey*: 'As Homer could introduce the perspectives of his own day into his picture of the material culture of his heroic world, so could he reflect, both directly and indirectly, the moral perspective of his own post-heroic age. The scope of the *Iliad*'s sympathies are capacious and generous. It contains two not always totally congruent worlds: that of the heroes and that of the poet.'[1]

But there is also another side to heroic morality. The heroic man must, in general, look after himself. If injury was done to him, then his status demanded that he should make good his loss by his own efforts; it was no good appealing to the gods. But in certain very specific contexts, such an appeal could be made. There are several types of offence, within the heroic system, which are thought likely to provoke Zeus' anger: the giving of crooked judgements; offences against suppliants; the breaking of oaths, or of the laws of hospitality. It is, I think, only in this limited area that we can find room for the application of a concept of 'justice' in the heroic society Homer depicts.[2] For the rest, there is only one rule that governs the actions of the hero: that *tīmē*, honour, must be maintained – although this would have included the fulfilment of obligations to one's family and followers, as well as more individualistic goals. Zeus' concern shows similar limitations: he will uphold the rules by which mankind lives, but otherwise he behaves much like a mortal king, and shows the same passionate interest in the maintenance of his honour and position.

Homer's own conception of justice is, as I have suggested, somewhat broader. (It is not clear that he possessed a general term for 'justice'; but the idea is there nevertheless.) There is no reason to think that the heroic values had disappeared altogether by his time; indeed Hesiod, composing only a little later than Homer, has still to complain about the hawkish behaviour of 'kings' in his society. But quite plainly the social constraints on behaviour have increased considerably. The gods' concern widens correspondingly; but they show little tendency to be bound in their own behaviour by the rules that they enforce among mankind. Zeus admits to pitying men: 'I care about them,' he says, 'although they are mortal' (*Iliad* XX 21). But that does not prevent him from bringing evil to them, for no apparent reason other than that he chooses to do so: he has two jars, as Achilles tells us, one of evil gifts, one of good; and men's fate is decided by his distribution (*Iliad* XXIV 527 *ff*.). A remark from the pseudo-Aristotelian *Magna Moralia*, written some five hundred years after the composition of the Homeric poems, would have been just as appropriate in the eighth century. 'It would be odd', the author says, 'if someone were to say that he loved Zeus' (1208 b 30). Relations between god and man, at least within the confines of Olympian religion, always retained a strictly commercial flavour: a necessary, though by no means a sufficient, condition of the gods' favour was the giving to them of honour, *tīmē*, through ritual sacrifice. The benevolent gods that Socrates and Plato believe in are quite untraditional.

Much the same attitudes as I have attributed to Homer are expressed by Solon, the Athenian legislator, around the beginning of the sixth century. 'Zeus is not quick to anger, like a mortal, over single actions; but a man who has wickedness in his heart does not escape his notice through all time, but assuredly is brought to light in the end. But one man pays immediately, another later; and those who escape themselves, and whom the oncoming *moira* of the gods does not touch – assuredly it comes later; guiltless, their children, or still later generations, pay for their deeds' (13. 25–32). Later on, in the same poem, Solon declares that man is always at the mercy of the gods; good and bad fortune come from them, and no one knows, when he begins on a venture, how it will turn out in the end. 'The man who tries to do his work with skill suddenly falls into great and bitter ruin; while to the man who works badly god gives great good fortune in everything, freeing him from his folly. There is no limit set to wealth that man can see; for those of us who now have most work withdouble the effort to increase it; but who could sate all? The immortals bestow gain on mortals, but destruction arises from it, which Zeus sends to punish them' (65 *ff.*). But the difficulty was that Zeus' distribution of good and evil often seemed incompatible with the idea that he was concerned with justice. Theognis, writing later in the century, takes him to task for this, in a light-hearted way. 'Zeus, my friend, I am amazed at you: you rule over all, having honour to yourself and great power; you well know the mind and passions of each man; and your might is highest of all, king. How then, son of Kronos, can you bring yourself in your wisdom to keep the wicked and the just man alike in the same *moira*, whether men's mind is turned to wisdom, or to wanton violence, relying on unjust deeds?' (373–80). In a second passage (731 *ff.*) Theognis questions the arrangement by which vengeance falls on the descendants of the unjust, if the unjust themselves escape punishment. In that case, he says, 'the doer gets away, and someone else then takes the consequences'. And why don't the just get the material rewards they deserve? Anyone observing all this will thumb his nose at the gods, and go off and make his fortune, while the just waste away in poverty. This is not, of course, what the author wants us to do. There is no real contradiction between what he says here and the solid morality we find elsewhere in the Theognidean corpus; the poet is merely savouring the paradox of his own beliefs. But he has identified some real problems, of a kind that were later to be explored in depth by the tragedians of the fifth century.

For Solon, it is clear that the concept of justice is closely connected with that of obedience to law (see especially fragment 4). By his time, the growth of the city-state had forced the expansion and systematization of the legal system (Solon was himself responsible for the wholesale reform of Athenian law); and it is plausible to suppose that the concept of justice too had become more sharply defined. There is now a general term for it, the classical term *dikaiosunē*.[3] But the main quality the term denotes was also recognized by Homer: the just man is essentially the one who refrains from unsolicited aggression. (This is, again, much the same as the Socratic-Platonic conception.) And in other aspects too the old ideas are retained. Legal punishment is seen as an instrument of divine justice, as it is even in the fifth century: in the *Eumenides*, for example, Aeschylus represents the court of the Areopagus as the human counterpart of the avenging Furies – and the association is certainly much more than symbolic. But the sophists, who form the subject of the next chapter, took a different view.

Chapter notes

1. *The Theme of the Mutilation of the Corpse in the Iliad*, Leiden 1971 (*Mnemosyne*, Supplement 17), p. 12.
2. The Homeric poems are, of course, not historical documents; but it is by now clear that the culture they describe bears at least some resemblance to a historical culture, namely the one existing in Greece around the time of the Trojan War (the event which forms the backdrop to both poems), some few centuries before they were composed. Their own date is now generally placed in the eighth century B.C.
3. In fact, this term is first attested only in Theognis, who is later than Solon; but Solon certainly uses the corresponding adjectives *dikaios, adikos* ('just', 'unjust') in the required general sense.

2 The sophists

The word *sophistēs* was originally a term for the expert craftsman, in whatever field (literally, the *sophistēs* is the possessor of *sophiā*, which is either 'expert skill', as here, or, more generally, 'wisdom': see Aristotle, *Nicomachean Ethics* 1141 a 9 *ff.*); but in the fifth century it came to be attached particularly to a class of professional teachers of *rhetoric*. (Many sophists also taught other subjects, but rhetoric seems to have been a common denominator.) It is this class which will be the subject of this chapter.

In the Platonic dialogue named after him, the sophist Protagoras is made to define his subject in the following way: ' "if [a pupil] comes to me, he will learn . . . prudence both about his private affairs and about the affairs of the city; how best to run his own household, and how to have the most influence on the affairs of the city in both speech and action" ' (318 e–319 a). In Aristotle's *Rhetoric*, Protagoras' claim is said to be that he can teach people to 'make the weaker argument the stronger'. Aristotle gives an example of the kind of technique involved: 'if a man is not open to the charge – for example, if he is a weakling charged with physical assault – the defence is that he was not likely to have done it. But if he *is* open to the charge – that is, if he is a strong man instead of a weakling – then the defence is still that he was not likely to have done it, because he could be sure that people would think he *was* likely to have done it' (*Rhetoric* 1402 a 18–20, in an adapted version of the Oxford translation). Together, these passages from Plato and Aristotle probably give a fair picture of Protagoras' aims as a teacher of rhetoric; and also, I think, of those of the sophists generally. What they promised their pupils was the key to success in political and forensic debate; and to judge from the high fees that the most prominent among them were able to charge, it was a commodity that was much in demand.

Their enemies – and there were many of them – claimed that they were merely tricksters and illusionists. I have already mentioned

Plato's opposition to them (in the introductory chapter). Aristotle's feelings are much the same; his conclusion about Protagoras, after the passage just quoted, is that 'people were justified in objecting to what [he] promised to teach; for it was deceit, and not genuine but only apparent probability' (*Rhetoric* 1402 a 25–7). Or again, take Xenophon's judgement: 'the sophists talk in order to deceive, and write for their own gain, and are of no benefit to anyone; for none of them is wise or ever became wise, but each of them is content to be called a sophist, which is a term of reproach, at any rate among men of sense. So my advice is to be on your guard against the teachings of the sophists, but not to despise the arguments of the philosophers' (Xenophon, *On Hunting*, 13. 8). But there is also a positive side to the sophists' activity, which tends to become obscured by the almost universal hostility of our sources about them; and that is that rhetoric, the art of speaking persuasively, is an indispensable feature of a democratic society, such as Athens was at that time (i.e. in the latter half of the fifth century). To be sure, it could be used as a means to personal aggrandizement; but it also provided the means by which responsible leaders could ensure acceptance of their policies. Similarly, on the forensic level, the innocent as well as the guilty require an effective defence. It is also perfectly possible that the strong arguments could be on the side of the guilty, and the weak on the side of the innocent; in that case, the ability to 'make the weaker argument the stronger' will be a positive boon to society. (What, for instance, if the strong man in Aristotle's example is actually innocent of the charge, but all the circumstantial evidence points to him?) Aristotle, at any rate, is perfectly well aware of the general point; and towards the end of his life even Plato admits that rhetoric has a role to play (see Ch. 6 below). It is also almost certainly true that the older sophists, like Protagoras, were honest men. According to Plato's account, Protagoras himself recognized the virtues of justice, self-control, and so on as necessary to continued social existence (my source, once again, is the dialogue *Protagoras*, especially 320 c–328 d), and, what is more, made them the basis of his teaching. Plato does not accuse Protagoras of immorality (and if he could have done, he would surely not have missed the opportunity); his quarrel with him is rather about his qualifications and his methods.

We probably have to distinguish between three different kinds of antagonism towards the sophists. Firstly, there is the antagonism of ordinary people, as illustrated by Aristophanes' comedy *Clouds*, which can no doubt be put down largely to the plain man's often justified suspicion of the intellectual élite. Secondly, there is the antagonism of the Athenian establishment, which we find expressed, for example, by the excellent Anytus in Plato's *Meno* (89 e *ff.*). Men like this perhaps saw the sophists as a potential threat to their own influence; they also had a certain aristocratic contempt for those who put out their services for hire. Thirdly, there is the antagonism of the philosophers, or at any rate of Socrates and Plato (the qualification is important, for many other philosophers, both later and contemporary, were in fact in close agreement with the sophists' approach).[1] It is, of course, the third kind of opposition that concerns us in the present context. The central reason for it was the generally sceptical attitude that was shared by the sophistic movement as a whole. This attitude seems to have derived largely from the preoccupation with rhetoric. Protagoras, according to Diogenes Laertius, held that 'there are two arguments on every subject that are opposed to each other' (IX 51); he also apparently wrote two books of *Counter-Arguments* (*Antilogiai*), which no doubt substantiated the point. These have not survived, but we do have an anonymous document which seems to belong to the same genre, the so-called *Dissoi Logoi,* or *Two-fold Arguments.* The author of this document begins by discussing certain pairs of concepts, (good, bad; fine, shameful; just, unjust; true, false): arguments are first put forward to show that the two members of each pair are identical, then to show that they are different. For example, 'Illness is bad for the sick but good for the doctors. And death is bad for those who die, but good for undertakers and grave-diggers'; on the other hand, 'I think that the man who says [that good and bad are the same] would be unable to answer, if anyone asked him, "Tell me, did your parents ever do you any good?" He would reply, "Yes, a great deal." "Then you owe them many great evils, if the good is the same as the bad" ' (1. 3, 12). It is only a short step from this kind of exercise to the Protagorean brand of scepticism. What is good for one man is bad for another; what is unjust in one set of circumstances is just in another; a wind which is cold to you is warm to me. The latter is an example used by Plato in the *Theaetetus* (151 e *ff.*) to illustrate Protagoras' notorious dictum, 'Man is the measure of all things, both of the things that are, that they are, and of the things that are not, that they are not.' What he seems to have meant by this (though not everyone would agree with this account) is that we have no access to the external world as it really is; we are all locked in the privacy of our own perceptions and beliefs, so that each of us becomes the 'measure' of how the world is for us. But there is probably also another meaning: that it is man – and not the gods – who creates the conditions of human life. 'About the gods', he said at the beginning of his work *On the Gods*, 'I have no means of knowing, either that they exist or that they do not exist [or what kind of form they have]; for there are many things that prevent me from knowing, the lack of evidence and the shortness of human life.' This fragment too is quoted by Diogenes *ibid.*, who continues: 'Because he began his treatise in this way, he was expelled by the Athenians, and they burned his books in the agora, having first collected them by means of proclamation from all who owned copies'. It is this humanistic element in his thinking that provides the link between his scepticism and his moral beliefs. 'Whatever things seem just and fine to each city *are* just and fine for that city, so long as it thinks them so' (attributed to Protagoras in the *Theaetetus*, 167 c). Different things, then, seem just and fine to different cities, so that we are prevented from establishing any fixed standards. On the other hand, he maintains that without rules of some kind, life would be intolerable; he also holds particular moral beliefs of his own, of a fairly traditional kind. His sceptical thesis does not debar him from this; nor does it debar him from trying to inculcate his beliefs in others, as we saw Plato making him claim to do in the *Protagoras* (Socrates understands him as promising to make men 'good citizens' [319 a]; *cf.* 322 e–323 a). But whether that claim was borne out in practice is perhaps another matter.

Gorgias, the famous stylist, also expressed sceptical sentiments. (As I said in the introductory chapter, he was, with Protagoras, probably the most influential of the sophists.) We have a set of arguments by him which purport to show three things: firstly, that nothing exists; secondly, that if anything does exist, it cannot be known; and thirdly, that if it can be known, the knowledge cannot be communicated (fr. 3). This is clearly intended as a parody of the arguments of the Eleatic philosophers, Parmenides and Zeno (whose conclusions, if more positive, were scarcely less odd); but it is at the same time also a quite serious demonstration of the principle enunciated by Protagoras, that for every argument there exists a counter-argument. In the exhibition speech *Encomium of Helen* we find the same sceptical approach applied in the ethical sphere. Gorgias here deliberately sets out to overturn common assumptions about human responsibility: 'I shall set out the causes through which it was likely that Helen's voyage to Troy should take place. She did what she did either by the will of Fate and the decision of the gods and the vote of Necessity, or else because she was seized by force, or because she was persuaded by words [or because she was possessed by love]. Now if it was through the first cause, it is right that the one who is being held responsible should be held so; for a god's will cannot be prevented by human forethought. . . . But if she was seized by force and illegally assaulted and unjustly outraged, it is clear that the one who did the forcing, as the aggressor, did the wrong, and the one who was forced, as the victim, did the suffering . . . But if it was speech that persuaded her and deceived her soul, it is not difficult to answer even this, and to free her from responsibility, in the following way. Speech is a great lord, which by means of the smallest and most invisible body effects the most divine results; for it can stop fear, take away grief, create joy, increase pity . . .' (there follows a long series of further illustrations of the power of speech). 'What reason therefore prevents us from thinking that Helen too, against her will, might have come under the influence of speech, just as if she had been seized by the force of those stronger than her?[2] . . . I shall discuss the fourth cause in my fourth argument. If it was love who did all this, there will be no difficulty in escaping the responsibility for the crime that is said to have been committed. For the things we see do not have the nature we wish them to have, but the one each actually has. . . . Because of the frightening things they have seen, people have momentarily taken leave of their wits; such is the way that fear extinguishes and drives out thought . . . So if Helen's eye, pleased by the figure of Paris, presented desire and conflict of love to her soul, what is there surprising in that? If, [being] a god, [love has] the divine power of the gods, how could one weaker than him reject him and drive him off?' (Gorgias, fr. 11, 5–19)[3]

But – again, by Plato's account – Gorgias' own moral stance, like Protagoras', was conventional. The same is not true of some of the younger, more extreme, sophists. Their position, however, is well represented in two of the Platonic dialogues that I shall be discussing in later chapters (i.e. the *Gorgias*, where the extremist view is defended by the perhaps imaginary Callicles, and the *Republic*, where Socrates crosses swords with the undoubtedly real Thrasymachus); and they can therefore safely be passed over here.

There is much that is of interest in the sophistic movement. Protagoras, in particular, is a striking figure (though unfortunately the hard evidence about him is relatively scanty). It would be wrong to overemphasize their importance, at least in the philosophical sphere; in the end their ideas are less valuable in themselves than for the replies they provoked. But it can be claimed for the sophists that their irreverent attitude towards traditional assumptions was the main stimulus towards the development of systematic ethical philosophy.

Chapter notes

1. I omit Aristotle's name at this point, although I have earlier mentioned him as sharing the Socratic-Platonic view of the sophists, because for him the term 'sophist' refers more to a type than to particular individuals; already, thanks largely to Plato's influence, 'sophistic' has come to be equivalent simply to 'fallacious'.
2. The text here is badly corrupted, but this clearly gives the right sense (the reconstruction is by Diels, in the standard edition of the fragments of the Presocratics: see Bibliography).
3. Scepticism for Gorgias is clearly more an attitude of mind than a developed theory; but the case may be different with Protagoras.

3 Socrates

Socrates is a peculiarly difficult subject. Since he wrote nothing, our knowledge of him depends entirely on reports about him by others. But there is also a considerable diversity in these reports: firstly, because of Socrates' (apparently) cryptic modes of expression; and, secondly, because he was the kind of man who inevitably evoked an emotional as well as an intellectual reaction. The evidence for this is not only the way in which the character Socrates affects his audiences in the Platonic dialogues (though Xenophon, in his *Memorabilia*, bears out at least this aspect of Plato's portrait); there is also the fascination that Socrates clearly continued to exercise over Plato himself until long after his death, and – perhaps most important of all – the fact of his trial and execution. That he could have been convicted on such general charges (impiety, and corrupting the young) seems to suggest an undercurrent of hostility towards him; and on the whole it is not likely that the grounds for this were political.

The difficulty of the evidence is not in itself a reason for dismissing Socrates from consideration. But when it is added to the fact that most of his ideas were evidently also accepted by Plato, at some time in his life, it is tempting to try at least to get along by treating the two of them together, scattering a few references to the historical Socrates in the footnotes. But I believe that in spite of all the difficulties it is still worth attempting to separate out Socrates' own specific contribution; not least because it would be a pity to lose sight of so colourful a figure. Unfortunately, the main source on which the reconstruction has to depend is Plato. It will be necessary, therefore, to preface the discussion of Socrates with a few brief remarks on the so-called 'Socratic problem': the problem, that is, about how to disentangle the real, historical Socrates from the Socrates who appears, usually in the leading role, in most of Plato's dialogues. It is now (so far as I know) universally accepted that Plato's Socrates at least at *some* stage becomes a mouthpiece for ideas which the historical Socrates either did not hold or could not have held. The basis for this is essentially Aristotle's testimony: Aristotle states quite categorically that Socrates did not subscribe to the so-called 'theory of forms' which Plato puts into his mouth in the *Phaedo, Republic,* and other dialogues. The question then is how much, if any, of what Plato attributes to him Socrates actually did believe. No very precise answers are possible; but unless we take the question seriously, then any claim that we are talking about *Socrates* will obviously be weakened.

Aristotle is often accused of being unreliable as a historian of philosophy, and with good reason; but his relatively few, short statements about Socrates are backed up to a considerable extent by other, independent, evidence. 'Two things', he says, 'can fairly be attributed to Socrates: inductive *logoi* [i.e. arguments based on the collection of instances] and universal definition' (*Metaphysics* 1078 b 27–9). Then follows the sentence to which I referred in the last paragraph: 'But Socrates did not make universals separate, nor did he make his definitions separate; while others [i.e. the Platonists] did separate them, and called such things ideas [forms] of the things that are.' The same interest in definition is shown by Xenophon's Socrates; and also by the Socrates of one particular group of Platonic dialogues, which in all probability belong to a relatively early period in Plato's career, and in which the theory of ideas does not figure: e.g. the *Charmides, Laches, Lysis.*

A standard feature of the early dialogues is that they end with an announcement by Socrates that he and his partners in the argument are really no better off than they were when they started; they still don't know the nature of temperance, or piety, or courage, or whatever is the subject of the argument. The claim of ignorance is one that Plato's Socrates frequently makes; and Aristotle has heard of it too: so he tells us that 'Socrates used to ask questions without giving answers; for he confessed that he didn't know the answers' (*Sophistici Elenchi* 183 b 7–8). It is true that Aristotle might here be relying on Plato; and support for that contention could perhaps be found in the fact that Xenophon's Socrates usually *does* know the answers. Yet clearly elsewhere Aristotle does not rely completely on the Platonic dialogues for his evidence about Socrates; if he did, he would not be able to deny Socrates a belief in separated forms. On balance, then, it seems plausible to regard the tone of the early dialogues as authentically Socratic. It looks significant, too, that the abandonment of this 'aporetic' tone is more or less contemporaneous with the introduction in the dialogues of the theory of forms.

On another point, Plato, Aristotle and Xenophon are again in agreement: Socrates' chief interest was in ethics. Plato represents him as having had an early interest in natural philosophy, which he abandoned on discovering that it could not give him the answers he wanted; Aristotle says simply that 'he busied himself with ethical matters, and with nature in general not at all' (*Metaphysics* 987 b 1–2). Xenophon says the same as Aristotle. The odd man out on this occasion is Aristophanes, whose *Clouds* caricatures Socrates as a scientist and teacher of rhetoric. It is clear, however, that Aristophanes' butt is not so much Socrates as the sophistic movement in general, with which Socrates would naturally have been associated in the popular mind. Enough in Aristophanes' portrait is authentic – details of dress, habits and so on – to make it recognizable; and that is all.[1]

The net result is that Plato's early works seem to represent the best source on Socrates' philosophical activities (and especially the *Apology*, in which he is made to give an account of his life). Aristotle's brief statements on the whole do no more than to help us to that conclusion; in themselves, they provide us only with the barest outline of Socrates' concerns – and, in one major respect, a distorted one. Mostly, his reports consist in isolated references, occurring wherever Socratic ideas are relevant to the subject in hand. Where there is more substantial discussion of Socrates, Aristotle tends to concentrate on two points: firstly, on how he avoided Plato's mistake of separating off universals from particulars; and, secondly, on how he himself made a fatal mistake in overrating the importance of knowledge for virtue. On this second point, I shall argue, Aristotle at least partially misunderstood Socrates. (My strategy here might seem to involve a somewhat perverse use of Aristotle: first to use him to legitimize Plato as a source, then to complain about the inadequacy of his evidence. But my complaint only affects some of his interpretative remarks about Socrates, not the plain factual statements I used in my argument.)

Unfortunately, although the early Platonic works are the best sources we have, their evidence is still not easy to interpret. Even here there is no complete and explicit exposé of Socratic ideas (and could scarcely be, at least in the dialogues, when they are apparently intended to portray the real Socrates, the master of ignorance. The

Apology initially looks more promising, but there too there are important gaps.) Instead, we are mostly brought back to the two notorious and problematic paradoxes, 'Virtue is knowledge', and 'No man does wrong willingly'. The following discussion of Socrates' ideas will consist largely in an attempt to discover the meaning of these two paradoxes (the second as well as the first is known to Aristotle, and is discussed by him at length). Because of the ambiguity of the evidence, I cannot claim certainty for my account. But I shall not be inclined to say for that reason – as Socrates might – that it is 'merely' the account in which I happen to believe; I believe it to be the correct one.

At the core of Socratic philosophy lies the method that is illustrated in the early Platonic dialogues: the 'elenchus', or the testing of people's views through questioning. (Typically, in these dialogues, a character proposes a definition of whatever is under consideration, which Socrates then proceeds to inspect).[2] In principle this testing is neutral; but in practice it almost always turns into refutation. For that reason, Socrates' approach often seems an essentially negative one. But at the same time, he claims to have a moral purpose in his questioning (this is nowhere clearer than in the *Apology*): and that is, to make men better men. Showing people that they don't know what courage is, or what temperance is – although they think they do know – is therefore evidently thought of as contributing in some way to their moral improvement. It is natural at this point to think of the first of the two paradoxes, 'Virtue is knowledge'. Virtue, so Socrates seems to say, is knowing what virtue is, what is virtuous; or in other words, know-ledge is a necessary and sufficient condition of being virtuous. Given that view – odd though it may appear – then one could see how showing people their ignorance might be thought of as connected with the business of improving them: only when they recognized that they didn't possess the requisite knowledge of virtue would they be likely to start looking for it. This is almost certainly the way in which Socrates thought. His final aims are wholly positive; only we rarely seem to get beyond the first, negative part of the process. Socrates himself is well aware of this criticism: thus it is that in the *Apology* he represents his life's work as an unsuccessful search for knowledge. No one has the knowledge he has looked for. If he is wiser than anyone else (as the Delphic oracle seemed to say), it is because he knows that he knows nothing. If we strip away the mythical or literary trappings of this story, it becomes a simple admission of failure – or at any rate of partial failure.

There is a strong temptation to suppose that what Socrates thought really important was not so much finding the answer to the question of the nature of virtue, as just being prepared to ask it: 'the unexamined life', he says, 'is unlivable for man' (*Apology* 38 a). The ideal itself may be in practice unattainable; what matters is that we should strive for it. It is then only a short step from this to saying that Socrates' vision is of man 'as a mature, responsible being, claiming to the fullest extent his freedom to make his own choice between right and wrong, not only in action, but in judgement' (Gregory Vlastos, 'The Paradox of Socrates', in *The Philosophy of Socrates: A Collection of Critical Essays*, p. 21). But it is extremely doubtful whether Socrates wants to allow us such freedom of choice. From most of the arguments in the 'Socratic' dialogues it is obvious that he has more than an inkling of the kind of standards he wants to maintain – or, in other words, that there are certain virtues, and that these have a single definition. Certainly, each man has to recognize the truth for himself; the knowledge that Socrates has in mind is not likely to have been the ability to parrot moral rules, but rather a question of *coming to see* that certain things are, e.g., just or courageous, or if you like, of relating moral rules to oneself (this is a crucial point, to which I shall return in a moment). But there is only one truth – whatever form it may take.

The purpose of the Socratic method, then, is to discover the nature of virtue. But just what does this involve? In other words, what is Socrates looking for when he asks for a definition? His strategy in different places suggests different answers: sometimes, for example, he seems to be searching for a universal rule, or set of rules, for virtuous action; sometimes the search is for the *essence* of virtue (put in the form of a request for what all the virtues, or what all the instances of one particular virtue have in common); sometimes merely for a way of distinguishing the thing being defined from other things. In the final analysis, however, there is little doubt that what Socrates is after is some means of deciding whether an action is virtuous or not. His fundamental question is, how should men behave? This then is naturally interpreted in terms of the categories of acceptable behaviour enshrined in the Greek language, and becomes: what is justice? courage? temperance?

The paradox 'virtue is knowledge' is quite certainly not itself intended as a definition, however elastic the notion of 'definition' may seem to be for Socrates. It is, perhaps, a slogan, which announces – as I suggested – that unless a man has knowledge, he cannot be virtuous; and also that if he has knowledge, he cannot not be virtuous. The slogan both reflects and advocates the Socratic method. (In the *Republic*, Plato himself effectively points out the absurdity of treating 'virtue is knowledge' as a definition – of whatever kind: subtle people, Socrates is made to say there, identify the good with wisdom; but they can't say what sort of wisdom it is, and are forced in the end to say that it is wisdom about the good [505 b].) But the question then arises, why Socrates should ever have put so much emphasis on the importance of knowledge; for it is quite implausible, on the face of it, to suppose that knowledge is either a necessary or a sufficient condition of virtue. Vlastos (in the essay I referred to earlier) points out, for instance, that courage doesn't seem to stand in the required relation to knowledge: people can be courageous without being able to give any account of their actions; and they can know there's nothing to be frightened of, and still be frightened. In that case, 'Virtue is knowledge' will be not merely paradoxical, but straightforwardly false. In the case of courage, knowledge may apparently have no role to play at all. But there is, I think, rather more to what Socrates is saying than this would allow.

We should begin by remembering what Socrates' overall purpose is: not to give an abstract analysis of virtue, but to contribute to men's moral improvement. In the early dialogues, we find him almost inevitably confronted with people whose beliefs he thinks confused, or actually mistaken, and wishes to put to rights (and it is just that point, that their beliefs are confused, that Socrates makes when he concludes a dialogue by saying that the whole argument has been fruitless; for it is on their beliefs – not Socrates' – that the search for a definition has been based). It is perhaps fairly obvious to suppose that it was his preoccupation with the business of persuasion that made him rate knowledge so high among the conditions for virtue. The very fact that it is possible to influence people's behaviour at all by reasoning with them shows that rational processes play a role in determining that behaviour; maybe then in his enthusiasm for argument Socrates overlooked the fact that other elements are involved too (Aristotle thinks he missed out desire or choice).

Against this criticism, there are two possible lines of defence that could be provided for Socrates. The first is to emphasize that 'virtue is knowledge' is a *deliberate* paradox; and to say that, as such, it may

B

very well not be intended to be taken as literally true – if such an equation could be said to have a literal sense. Socrates could be saying just that knowledge is important, not that it is the only factor. But even if this would work, it looks suspiciously like a whitewash. The second defence is more hopeful, and more interesting. We need here to consider more directly what virtue is knowledge *of*. I earlier interpreted the request for a definition of virtue as a request for an answer to the question 'How should I act in order to act courageously, temperately, piously?' The knowledge in question will be partly knowledge of this. But it is also knowledge of *the good*, that is, knowledge of what is good for oneself – and that means knowing that acting courageously, temperately, or piously is good in that sense, and that acting in a cowardly, intemperate, or impious way is bad. Exactly how these things are supposed to be good or bad for one is a question that will be raised later; for the moment, I want to consider the relation between the two kinds of knowledge. Sometimes one is emphasized more than the other: the first, when the discussion is about one particular virtue; the second, when the topic is the importance of virtue itself. But essentially they are the two sides of a single coin. If we know, in the proper sense, what courage is, then we know that we ought to do this or that, and so that it is good to do it. In effect, the second kind of knowledge marks the distinction between moral knowledge, knowing that one ought to do something, and factual knowledge, knowing that something is the case; the difference being that knowing that one ought to do something involves some kind of commitment to *action*.

One immediate problem is that Socrates claims that someone who knows what's right can't act otherwise. In the *Protagoras*, he seems to endorse the view that 'knowledge [i.e. moral knowledge] is a fine thing and capable of governing man, and if someone recognizes what is good and what bad, he will not be overcome by anything, so as to do anything other than what his knowledge tells him to do' (352 c). This is certainly not part of our conception of moral knowledge: knowing that one ought to do something would normally be thought of as quite compatible with not doing it. There are two reasons for the difference. The first is that – as the *Protagoras* passage shows – knowledge is thought of as being in itself unshakable (in contrast with thinking or believing something: one can be argued out of one's beliefs). The second reason is that Socrates holds that no one can knowingly act against his best interests; thus, since knowing what's right involves knowing it to be best for one, right action must inevitably follow. (The idea that no one can knowingly do something that harms him is sometimes treated as a paradox in its own right; but unlike 'Virtue is knowledge' or 'No man does wrong willingly' it is not altogether implausible as a general statement, and the characters in the Platonic dialogues find little difficulty in accepting it.) The result is that in cases where someone seems to act 'against his better knowledge', Socrates is forced to question the state of mind of the agent: did he *really* know it would be bad for him? (Did he really *know* it was wrong?) Didn't he just make a wrong assessment, which he later regretted? The move has at least some chance of success, since the actual behaviour of the agent will always be an important part of the evidence about the beliefs that he holds. Someone who says that he knows he shouldn't do a particular thing, but does it repeatedly, is likely to find his claim treated with some scepticism. But the same clearly wouldn't be true in the case of a man who abandoned his normally high standards of behaviour on one solitary occasion: his cry of 'I don't know what came over me' would surely provide the perfect counter-example to Socrates' position. But that position is still much stronger than is apparent at first sight. If a man could really know that doing what was right was best for him, then under normal circumstances we would expect him to do it. What is beyond doubt is that Socrates did not think that the mere possession of a set of definitions would make one virtuous. (This is what Aristotle accuses him of in *Eudemian Ethics* I 5; and probably also in *Nicomachean Ethics* VI 13.)

The second paradox, 'No man does wrong willingly', is very closely related to the first. If those who do wrong do so unwillingly, they must do it either through ignorance or under compulsion (see Aristotle, *Nicomachean Ethics* III 1-2. The analysis, which seems slightly odd in English, is possible in Greek because the words *hekōn* and *ākōn* do double duty: they cover not only 'willingly', 'un-willingly', but 'intentionally', 'unintentionally' – which naturally makes them very difficult to translate). Because of the emphasis that Socrates puts on knowledge, it seems overwhelmingly likely that he has just the first alternative in mind: vice is unwilling because it is the result of ignorance. And this very point is directly implied by the first paradox. If the man who has knowledge cannot act viciously (because his knowledge includes the knowledge that virtue is best for him, and he cannot act against his best interests), then the man who does act viciously can only do so because he lacks knowledge. No one wants to harm himself; thus, Socrates argues, no one 'really wants' to do wrong. Plenty of people want to do what is in fact wrong, but without *knowing* that it is wrong. They may know that others *call* it wrong, but they cannot themselves be said to know its wrongness (because if they did, they would act accordingly). (Thus, Socrates' real concern is not with those who supposedly 'act against their better knowledge' in the sense that they do things they would normally refrain from doing, but rather with those who regularly behave in a vicious way. They too could be described as 'knowingly' doing wrong; but in fact, Socrates says, this is a misdescription: if they did know it was wrong, they wouldn't do it – because of what moral knowledge is. But cases of the first sort will still be a difficulty for him.)

From what I have said so far, it is obvious that much of Socrates' position depends on his being able to make good sense out of the claim that vice is harmful, and virtue beneficial. This is what under-pins the view that knowledge is a sufficient condition of virtue; and also the idea that those who do wrong do not do what they 'really want'. Now it is possible that Socrates means that vice is harmful in the sense that it causes material loss, loss of respect, and so on;[3] and one could in fact make a fairly strong case on those lines. But the trouble is that it is a wholly contingent matter whether vicious behaviour will be harmful in this literal sense; it would therefore be implausible to treat it as something that one could be certain about, as Socrates is committed to doing. The harmfulness of vice must be something *inevitable*. Punishment after death could perhaps be made to fit this requirement; after all, divine justice might be expected to lack the deficiencies of human justice. Probably Socrates did believe in the possibility of an after-life. But if so, he lacked the certainty that Plato feels about it. In the *Apology*, he is openly agnostic: 'either the dead are nothing and have no consciousness of anything, or else it is, as people say, a change of place for the soul from here to another place' (but in either case it is likely to be a good thing) (40 c). Earlier in the same work, he complains about those who pretend that they know what death will bring: 'No one knows if it may not even be the greatest of goods, but as it is they are afraid of it as if they had full knowledge that it was the greatest of evils. . . . If I were to claim to be wiser in any respect than anyone else, it would be in this, that not having sufficient knowledge about the things in Hades, I recog-nize that I don't possess this knowledge' (29 a–b). If he had made his argument depend on the assumption of divine retribution after death, he would surely have been guilty of the same mistake of which he here accuses others.

The key to the true meaning of Socrates' claim that vice is harmful to us is contained in a standing analogy that he makes between vice and disease. Men possess a thing called 'soul', which like the body can be either in good condition or in bad condition. Its good condition, which corresponds to health in the body, is virtue; its bad condition is vice. Thus, vice is supposed to be harmful to the soul in a way similar to that in which disease is harmful to the body. (Hence Socrates' continual exhortation to us to 'care for our souls'.)

In order to understand *this*, we need to know something more about Socrates' use of the word 'soul' (or, rather, *psuchē*: it goes without saying that we should not prejudge the question of the overlap between the Greek and English words; but at any rate 'soul' seems to have more in common with *psuchē* than does any other single English word). Since the word is used in the early dialogues without analysis or explanation (not so, of course, in later dialogues, like the *Phaedo* or *Republic*), it seems plausible to suppose that Socrates used it in a fairly ordinary way, i.e. that his use corresponded pretty well with the everyday usage of his contemporaries. Earlier and contemporary literature shows that the word had a wide range of meaning: life; the gibbering shade in Hades; the 'immortal soul' of Pythagoreanism or the mystery religions; the 'inner man'. Obviously, though, we can dismiss the first two senses: either would make nonsense of the injunction to 'care for the soul'. We are left, then, with the last two. But these, again, are probably intimately connected: the 'soul' that is supposed to survive death is no doubt not so very different from the 'inner man', or, if you like, the 'mind', or a man's thoughts and emotions. It is something like this that Socrates means by 'soul' (we should not, I think, try to press him any harder).

We are, of course, perfectly familiar with the notion of a 'diseased mind'. But Socrates' notion is rather different. Our normal assumption would be that someone who is mentally diseased is suffering from a condition that is actually treatable by a doctor; that is to say, mental disease is literally a kind of disease. Even when the term is extended to the criminal mentality, the same assumption remains. But Socrates' position is only that vice is *like* disease, not that it *is* disease. 'Having vice in one's soul' means being in a bad condition morally; having a disease means being in a bad condition physically.

The analogy is by no means an implausible one. Vice, like disease, can be 'cured' (by punishment). Again, it is at least sometimes painful in itself, e.g. when a person feels guilt or remorse. We might also argue that vice is like disease in that it limits our capabilities: just as disease interrupts our lives, and prevents us from doing the desirable things that we do when healthy, so perhaps vice prevents us from doing certain other desirable things. And this line of argument might produce a reasonably clear sense in which vice could be said to be harmful. But it is not, I think, a line that Socrates himself followed up. What he stresses is the importance of possessing virtue, being in a virtuous condition, rather than that of doing virtuous things. (Probably, this is because of his moralistic purpose: his primary goal is the recovery of the patient.) My own view is that he relied for the purposes of his argument on the general point that vice and disease are both undesirable things, things to be avoided, and went no deeper than that.

Socrates holds not merely that vice is harmful, but that it is more damaging than anything else. Conversely, virtue is supremely beneficial: provided we have virtue, even the worst misfortune cannot touch us. This might be called the third Socratic paradox: the paradox of the invulnerability of virtue. 'There is no evil', Socrates says at the end of the *Apology*, 'that can happen to the good man either in life or in death' (41 d). Earlier, he suggests a rather less extreme position: 'My business is to persuade you . . . not to care for your bodies or your property before your soul, or so much . . . ; virtue does not come from wealth, but from virtue comes wealth and all other goods' (30 a–b). This implies that virtue is valuable as a means to external goods (though, of course, it could be valuable in other ways at the same time – and indeed must be: it would be impossible for Socrates to say in the same breath that virtue is beneficial simply because it leads to material benefits, and that souls are more important than bodies), in which case external goods matter as well as virtue. If so, there are misfortunes that can happen to the good man, though they might be nothing compared with the misfortune of being vicious.

In any case, Socrates is tied to the view that the essential aspect of man is his aspect as a moral agent (since happiness lies in caring for one's soul, and caring for one's soul involves simply living virtuously). (His use of 'soul' therefore does show this difference from ordinary usage, that the 'inner man' is equated with a man's moral condition.) Someone who is vicious, he wants to say, is far less enviable even than the man with a diseased body, because his moral condition matters far more than his physical condition. But what reason does he give us for wanting to agree with him? What reason does he give us even for thinking virtue (i.e. the behaviour he calls virtuous) desirable, let alone for thinking it more desirable than anything else? The analogy between vice and disease we can either accept or reject; for though there are some things that vice has in common with disease, Socrates has done nothing to show that the two things are alike in the most important respect, namely in respect of undesirability. Vice is painful to some people; but what are we to do with someone who doesn't find it so – the very person Socrates is addressing? Almost all that we are left with is Socrates' own intense personal conviction; plus the fact that he evidently managed to live a life that was consistent with his main contention, that is, a life that was both virtuous and happy.[4] Perhaps this last point in itself gives him some claim on our attention. But it scarcely amounts to very much, since men have lived different sorts of lives, and still been happy.

But of course we must not forget that Socrates himself regarded 'mere belief', however strongly held, as quite inadequate. Whether or not his ultimate ambition was realizable – I mean that of finding universally valid reasons for what he believed – is a large question. At least, people still nourish the same ambition; and in general, even if the ideal of certainty turned out to be illusory, it would still be important that moral beliefs should be rationally supported. The mere fact of his insistence on the need for reason and argument would by itself make Socrates worth remembering.

Chapter notes

1. There are certainly some similarities of a general kind between Socrates and the sophists: for example, his interest in argument, and the destructive tendencies of his method (see pp. 31–2). But the differences are in the end more significant.
2. There is a good illustration of Socratic method in Book I of the *Republic*, which is discussed in Chapter 5. (The book follows the form of the early dialogues very closely; and some have concluded that it was itself originally an early work, written independently of the *Republic*.)
3. There is some support for this view in a passage at *Apology* 30 a–b (discussed on p. 38).
4. For Plato's fullest portrait of Socrates, see *Symposium* 215 a *ff*. The picture is, of course, idealized, but probably not too far from the truth.

4 Plato's 'Gorgias'

Every one of Plato's dialogues has something to say that is of relevance to ethics. But I shall be considering only four, with occasional reference to others. These four, the *Gorgias, Republic, Statesman,* and *Laws*, are the most important for an understanding of Plato's moral philosophy, and of the way in which it developed. The *Gorgias* is generally regarded as an early work; but for reasons that I shall give in a moment, I do not think that it can be separated very sharply from the dialogues of the middle period of Plato's life, and in particular from the *Republic*. These latter dialogues, broadly speaking, show Plato developing distinctive ideas of his own, although clearly always conscious of his Socratic model. The *Statesman* and *Laws*, on the other hand, probably represent a rather later stage in his career, one of the main features of which was a thorough rethinking of earlier views. The Platonic corpus is genuinely dialectical: in other words, it shows Plato debating with himself and with others, and in the course of the process continually modifying what he thought, both within individual dialogues, and between them. Of course, there are certain beliefs to which Plato held throughout his life. But like Socrates, he is not easily satisfied. (So, as we shall see, in the *Gorgias*, he begins to claim conclusiveness for his arguments, but then at once qualifies his triumph: the arguments tie Callicles [Socrates' main opponent in the dialogue] with adamantine chains – 'or so at any rate it seems as things stand now'. And then the debate is taken up again in the *Republic*, with a different opponent.) Sometimes he gives the appearance of being dogmatic; but the appearance is false. The forcefulness with which he states his ideas is largely a reflection of the earnestness of his moral purposes. It certainly does not mean that he will stand by those ideas through thick and thin; he will stand by them only so long as he sees a possibility of defending them. The real difference between him and Socrates is that he gets beyond the destructive stage of the 'elenchus' to construct something positive of his own, however tentatively.

Two problems need to be mentioned here. The first is that it is often very difficult to see how much of what is said by his characters Plato himself wishes to endorse. We cannot straightforwardly suppose that his position is always the one represented by Socrates; for Plato's Socrates, like the historical one, is full of 'irony' and dissimulation. Fortunately, though, this problem can be made to fall away, if we merely cease to insist on extracting a *system* from the Platonic dialogues. The dialogues (or at any rate most of them) must be read as *conversations*, not as elaborately stage-managed treatises. Each position represented is intended to be weighed by us, as it is weighed by the parties to the discussion; and the conclusions that finally emerge are supposed to be thought of not as the products of a single mind, but rather as the agreed results of a many-sided argument, in which the reader himself has been a participant. This is the reason why Plato himself never appears as a character in any of his dialogues: he means our concern to be not merely with what *he* thinks, but with the argument itself. And the conclusions are like the conclusions of a real conversation, in that they are always to some extent tentative, or approximate, because they have been reached in one particular context, and by one particular set of arguments; thus they can readily be set aside again, and the issues reopened.

The second problem concerns the much-debated issue of the so-called 'unwritten doctrines' of Plato. Aristotle in his *Metaphysics* attributes many doctrines to Plato of which there is little trace in the dialogues (the expression 'unwritten doctrines' is itself Aristotle's); and from this fact, together with some other evidence, has been derived the idea that what we find in the dialogues is not really the quintessential Plato – he, supposedly, is to be found elsewhere, mainly in the number-theory talked about in Aristotle's *Metaphysics*. The most important supporting pieces of evidence for this theory are two passages, one in the *Phaedrus* and one in the *Seventh Letter* (if that is genuine), in which Plato complains of the inadequacy of the written word in comparison with the spoken word. The general conclusion to which these passages point is that speech is the only proper medium for philosophy: the written word – and the criticism presumably applies to what Plato himself writes – cannot answer back, and is really only useful as an *aide-mémoire*. But in fact this theory, if correct (and a reasonably plausible case has thus far been made for it), would certainly not take any of the point away from an examination of the dialogues, firstly, because they are clearly intended as philosophical works, and contain arguments which call for discussion; and secondly because (to judge by the omens) what we might learn about the quintessential Plato could well be rather less interesting than what we have in the dialogues – especially in the sphere of moral philosophy. Hence the 'unwritten' Plato, for the purposes of this book, need not concern us.

The adoption of Socrates as his main character is symbolic of the relation of Plato's philosophy to Socrates'. Plato would probably have been inconceivable without Socrates. But what he takes over from him is reinforced, extended, and in some cases takes an entirely new shape. (Here, of course, I am talking essentially of the dialogues of the middle and later periods.) In ethics, Plato's main thrust is to provide the kind of backing for Socrates' central ideas which they lack in their original context. But as we shall see this leads him deep into two fields which Socrates himself seems to have left alone: metaphysics and politics. The three strands of ethics, politics, and metaphysics are inextricably entwined in Plato. Generally speaking, his political proposals provide the practical means for the realization of his moral ideals, while his metaphysics provides their theoretical basis. At least, this is a fair characterization of what we find in the *Republic*; the situation in the *Statesman* and *Laws* is rather more complicated.

The *Gorgias*, with which I begin, contains no metaphysics. Its main part is an attempt to answer the claim made by Callicles (and earlier by another character, Polus) that injustice, and not justice, is the key to happiness. This is a perfectly good Socratic theme; and there is little in the arguments laid out by Plato's Socrates in the dialogue which would be actually incompatible with what we know about the real Socrates. What makes it plausible to regard the dialogue as Platonic rather than Socratic is above all its tone: Socrates is far more assertive than we would expect him to be, and towards the end even shows signs of arrogance. (Of course, *all* the dialogues are Platonic to some degree; what I mean is that the *Gorgias* contains much more of Plato, much less of Socrates, than the 'Socratic' dialogues.) His behaviour is in general very like that of the 'Socrates' of the middle dialogues, who knows a good deal, and is ready to reveal it. Two more particular arguments: firstly, the *Gorgias* makes positive use of a belief in the survival of the soul after death, which I have argued that the historical Socrates would have been unlikely to do; secondly, there is a striking overlap between the argument of the

Gorgias and that of the *Republic* (to such an extent, in fact, that I am inclined to regard the *Gorgias* as a first sketch for the *Republic*).

There are three conversations in the *Gorgias*: between Socrates and Gorgias, Socrates and Polus, and Socrates and Callicles. The chief link between them is that Polus and Callicles are intended to exemplify the effects of the kind of rhetorical education that Gorgias offers. By the end of the first part of the dialogue, Socrates has forced Gorgias into saying that the orator must know the difference between right and wrong; and that if his own pupils don't happen to know it, then he'll teach them (460 a). Socrates even manages to reach the paradoxical conclusion that the orator will never do wrong, which is what stings Polus (whose name is the Greek for 'colt') to charge into the argument. Both Polus and Callicles, products of the new education, show the emptiness of Gorgias' statement that he'll teach his pupils about right and wrong (we know in any case that, unlike other sophists, Gorgias did not profess to teach virtue; this from *Meno* 95 c): Polus tries hard to be immoral, Callicles has slightly more success. Plato saw a natural connection between rhetoric and the rejection of ordinary moral standards; and as we saw in Chapter 2, there were some grounds for this view. The idea provides the central theme of the dialogue. (In particular, rhetoric is thought of as offering the means to the achievement of immoral ends.) As becomes clear in the discussion with Polus (though the point is hinted at earlier, e.g. at 458 a–b, where Socrates says that 'to hold a false opinion about the subject we are now considering is in my view the greatest evil that can befall a man'), the dispute about rhetoric is really only part of a much larger issue: the nature of happiness. Socrates, of course, holds that happiness consists in virtue; rhetoric, throughout, is associated with the opposite view, that happiness consists in vice.

Gorgias himself is treated with elaborate politeness by Socrates;[1] and on the whole it seems fair to accept this as a reflection of a certain respect for him on Plato's part (this is the usual view). At the same time, Plato makes Gorgias praise his skill in much the same terms as his acolyte Polus, for whom he evidently has no respect at all: so at 452 d, Gorgias says that rhetoric 'provides what is in truth the greatest of all goods: the thing which gives mankind in general its freedom, and each individual the possibility of ruling over others in his own state' (that is, the ability to persuade). In order to make sense of this extraordinary statement, I think we have to assume that freedom is meant to be the same thing as having the possibility of controlling others – everyone has the opportunity to learn rhetoric, and if he does, then he can avoid being dictated to by others, and dictate to them instead. This is borne out by Gorgias' following speech, in which he claims that the orator can make the doctor, the athletic trainer, and the businessman (*chrēmatistēs*, the man whose occupation is making money) his slaves, because he has the ability to sway the masses. Later on, Gorgias adds that of course there is a right way and a wrong way to use rhetoric; but the teachers of it teach it on the understanding that it will be used for just ends (456 e). Polus does not make this crucial qualification; but it has also appeared rather late in Gorgias' own account.

Socrates' criticism of Gorgias is that he contradicts himself (457 e, 461 a). During the course of the argument, Gorgias has identified rhetoric as being persuasion about 'the things that are just or unjust' (454 b). Socrates claims that he assumed when Gorgias said this that 'rhetoric could never be anything unjust, seeing that it is always making its speeches about justice'; and so he was surprised when Gorgias suggested that it could be used for unjust purposes (460 e–461 a). What underlies Socrates' criticism here is the old paradox, 'Virtue is knowledge'. He assumes that the orator who tries to persuade a jury on matters of justice must *know* about justice, in the same way as the teacher of mathematics who tries to 'persuade' us about mathematics (*cf.* 453 d–e) must know mathematics himself. But someone who knows about justice must be just. Gorgias agrees explicitly that the orator must know about justice at the end of the discussion (at 460 a); but Socrates clearly thinks of him as being committed to the point even before then (since he begins his accusation of inconsistency before 460 a). The reason why Socrates thinks this is that Gorgias has accepted analogies between rhetoric and skills like medicine and building; and just as the doctor and the builder know about their subject-matter, so then will the orator – his subject matter being, supposedly, 'the things that are just or unjust'. This is, of course, unfair to Gorgias, who actually said that rhetoric was about *persuasion*; justice and injustice came in only as the things the orator attempted to persuade people about. Thus if the analogy is to hold good the orator needs only to know about persuasion, not about justice. In that case, Gorgias could have rejected Socrates' criticism, at least before 460 a; he could have insisted that a man *doesn't* need to know about justice to be an orator, but that he will need to know about it if he is to put his skill to proper use. He could also have gone on to say that he cared so much about how his pupils used it that he would teach them, even though this really wasn't part of his function as teacher of rhetoric. But as I suggested before, Plato wants us to take Gorgias' real position to be the limited one he expresses at the beginning: that he merely teaches a technique, and that he himself cannot fairly be held responsible if it is misused by his pupils. This is the position that Plato wants to attack; and he has good reason to do so. Gorgias defends himself by making analogies with the athletic trainer, and the man who teaches people how to fight in full armour (456 c *ff.*): if a man learns skills from these and then misuses them, this shouldn't be a reason for taking against his teachers and expelling them from the city, because 'they imparted their skills to be used justly, in self-defence against enemies and criminals'. But this ignores the point that a training in rhetoric is claimed to give a man vast power: the power to do anything he likes, even to the point of taking over the city. The damage that could be done by a mad boxer or hoplite would be small in comparison. (One could add that the orator will also supposedly be immune against punishment, as the boxer and the hoplite will not.) Thus the teacher of rhetoric (if we accept the claims that Gorgias makes) must bear much greater responsibility than the athletic trainer.

There is a substantive point at issue here. An obvious parallel to Plato's picture of the orator, striking at the roots of civilized life, would be the scientist who in the honest pursuit of knowledge happens upon a new and ingenious means for the destruction of life. Like Gorgias, he might disclaim all responsibility for the use others made of his results; he, like any other scientist, was simply publishing in the interests of science. But of course he is not like any other scientist, any more than Gorgias is like any other teacher; both know that what they are doing may have disastrous consequences, and although the responsibility would be shared, whatever happens could not have happened – or might not have happened – without them. It is not difficult to sympathize with Plato's opposition to Gorgias here; though the argument he uses against him, as I have suggested, is of questionable value.

Polus reacts strongly to Socrates' idea that the orator will do no wrong: 'Do you *really* think rhetoric is like that?' (461 b). Socrates has merely shamed Gorgias into submission, for 'who do you think will deny that he knows what is just and will teach it to others?' So at once we are back where we were: being an orator does *not* involve knowing about justice. Socrates proceeds to expand on this. Polus asks him what sort of skill *he* thinks rhetoric is (since he evidently thinks Gorgias at a loss about it); and Socrates replies that he doesn't regard it as a skill at all. We have been well prepared for this point. It is not a skill, because it does not involve knowledge; it's a mere knack – it pretends to know what is best, but in fact is no more than an ability to titillate, acquired by experience. As cookery pretends to know what food is best for the body, while medicine actually knows, so rhetoric pretends to know what is healthy for the soul, which is something that belongs only to 'justice'. Cookery isn't a skill, 'because it has no rational understanding of the nature of the patient or the prescrition' (465 a; Dodds's text and translation). In general, Socrates says, 'anything that is irrational I refuse to call a skill'. Clearly, rhetoric too is supposed to be 'irrational' in this way. One could respond, much as I did earlier, by saying that rhetoric will in fact be able to give a perfectly good account of itself, as a set of techniques of persuasion. Socrates' description of the 'knack' of cookery is of a hit-and-miss affair; and quite obviously rhetoric isn't like that. But this objection does not affect the main thrust of Socrates' attack (I refer here mainly to the long speech 464 b–466 a), which is directed against the *deception* that is involved in rhetoric. He calls it a species of flattery: telling men what they want to hear, rather than what is best for them. This is the point that is taken up by Polus: 'So you think good orators are regarded as contemptible, as mere flatterers?' (466 a) Socrates replies with the familiar distinction between what people think they want, and what they really want: orators and tyrants (a conjunction first hinted at by Gorgias) have no power because they lack knowledge of what is best. (As the argument stands, they might in fact have power, because they might be doing what is best by accident. But Plato is already assuming that what is best is what is just, and orators and tyrants in Plato by definition act unjustly.) Socrates taunts Polus to refute him, but Polus doesn't understand what is meant. At this point, Socrates begins to reveal his whole position, in as paradoxical a fashion as possible, while being careful to get Polus' agreement to the general notion that the mere brute exercise of power isn't something good in itself: killing people, exiling them, and stealing their money *could* turn out to be disadvantageous, though Polus naturally laughs at Socrates when he claims that such things are disadvantageous when they're done *unjustly* (470 c). He laughs even louder when Socrates suggests that the man who's punished for his crimes is better off than the man who isn't (473 b *ff.*). Socrates replies that laughter is no substitute for refutation; then, when Polus claims that no one on earth would accept what he says, and that this is refutation enough, Socrates makes the most paradoxical statement of all: that in fact not only he, but Polus and everyone else really believes that doing an injustice is worse than suffering it, and not being punished worse than being punished.

Socrates now turns to the offensive. The basis of his argument is provided by the following exchange. Socrates: 'Which is worse, doing an injustice or suffering one?' Polus: 'Suffering one.' S.: 'Which is the more shameful?' P.: 'Doing an injustice.' S.: 'So doing an injustice is also worse, if more shameful?' P.: 'Not at all.' S.: 'I understand: you don't identify fine with good and shameful with bad.' P.: 'No' (474 c–d). Socrates then gets Polus' agreement to the notion that whatever is fine is called so either because it is useful or because it gives pleasure, or both; and that whatever is shameful is called so either because it is harmful or because it gives pain, or both. Doing an injustice is not more painful than suffering one; if it is more shameful, it must therefore be worse. Socrates then adds a slightly longer argument to prove his second main point, that paying the penalty for injustice is better than not paying it.

This is a slippery passage to get hold of. Polus declares that to commit injustice is more shameful than to suffer it, but better (more advantageous). Plato replies with a question: what exactly do we mean when we say that one thing is more shameful than another? After going through some examples, he suggests an answer: a thing is shameful (or ugly: the Greek word *aischron* covers both meanings) either because it causes pain (e.g. ugly things, to the eye or ear) or because it brings disadvantage, or both. Polus is apparently persuaded by Socrates' examples to accept this equation: 'That's a fine definition, Socrates,' he says at 475 a, 'to make fineness a matter of pleasure and the good'. The admission is, of course, fatal. But it is not immediately obvious why Polus should have made it; the survey of examples is, to say the least, not particularly impressive. There seem to be two alternatives. The first is that we are supposed to think that Polus really hankers after the idea that in fact committing injustice is more admirable as well as more advantageous than suffering it – and indeed Callicles is later to suggest that this is what Polus wanted to say; but there is no indication of it in the present passage. The second alternative, which I think more likely, is that Plato simply mistook the force of his examples. In this case, Plato himself accepts Socrates' definition (probably 'definition' should here be taken less than strictly; what Plato accepts is that what is morally good [fine] is beneficial, not that anything beneficial is morally good). His point against Polus, then, is that he is fundamentally confused: it is just self-contradictory to say that a thing is more shameful and more advantageous, because if it is shameful, it is *ipso facto* disadvantageous. (If Plato *does* accept Socrates' definition, then he is evidently committed to the idea that there are only two things that provide reasons for action, the pleasant and the beneficial [though later on, at 500 a, these are reduced to one: even pleasures, Socrates suggests, are embarked on with an eye to what is good for us]. This is somewhat surprising, for it seems to imply that Plato excludes the possibility that someone can do something because it is *right*; it also suggests that he excludes the possibility of altruism. I propose to postpone discussion of these points until the next chapter; for the moment I shall content myself with saying that I do not think that in the end Plato wishes to exclude at least the first possibility.)

But from Socrates' earlier claim, that everyone really agrees with him (474 b), it is clear that the argument is intended to have universal application. In so far as *anyone* says that doing wrong is more shameful than suffering it (and by definition almost everyone will say it, since it is a reflection of conventional morality), he is bound to say that it is worse. The trouble for Plato is that there are then two alternatives: either a person must stop saying that suffering wrong is worse, or he must stop saying that doing wrong is shameful; and on the face of it, given no account of just *how* doing wrong is worse, he has no very good reason for choosing the first alternative – especially when so much has been made of the attractions of injustice. In the conversation with Callicles, who chooses the second alternative, Plato begins to provide some such account.

Callicles, then, does not think that doing wrong is shameful; rather he regards it as exemplifying true virtue, or in other words, 'natural' as opposed to 'conventional' justice. The man who has the intelligence and courage needed for a really successful life of 'injustice' lives as a man should; any other form of life involves submitting oneself to the will of others, and is therefore slavish. One other condition of success will be the acquisition of political power; and the means to this lies in rhetoric. On the individual level, Callicles stands for the single-minded pursuit of pleasure; on the political level, he is recommending a kind of meritocracy, in which merit is measured by one's success at getting whatever one wants, by whatever means. (This is not thought of as necessarily involving the overthrow of existing society; the demagogue under a democracy as well as the tyrant would fit Callicles' criteria.)

I shall deal first with Socrates' strategy against Callicles. Callicles begins with a forceful statement of his own position. He says he will not be shamed into defeat as Polus was – claiming, I think falsely, that Polus really meant only that doing wrong is conventionally more shameful than suffering it. Socrates welcomes this promise of plain speaking, and says that Callicles will be his touchstone: with all his qualifications, any agreement between the two of them 'will really have achieved the goal of truth' (487 e). What Socrates says here is loaded with irony, but at the same time it clearly signals the fact that Callicles represents the main target of Plato's attack.

The first move is to establish more precisely what Callicles' meaning is. In effect, he has proposed that 'the stronger' should rule. For 'stronger', under prompting from Socrates, he now proceeds to substitute 'better' (489 c), then 'more intelligent and manly (courageous)' (491 b). True virtue, and true happiness, he sums up at 492 c, lie in being able to enjoy complete luxury and freedom with impunity. The man without needs, he says, is like a stone or a corpse. Socrates replies with an image of his own: someone who lives in the way that Callicles recommends is like one of those birds that excretes as fast as it can eat (494 b). And does it not matter what a man's wants are? If a man liked to scratch himself, would he be happy if his whole life were spent in scratching? Or are there some desires or pleasures that Callicles would want to exclude? What about a life of extreme sexual debauchery (the Greek word seems to have a more specific meaning, but I am unable to discover what that meaning is)? Callicles is shocked, and says that Socrates ought to be ashamed of introducing such subjects into the discussion. Socrates then asks him to make clear whether or not he really wants to identify pleasure and the good (i.e. whether or not he really holds, as he has implied, that things are to be pursued just in so far as they are pleasant); to which he replies that in order not to contradict himself, he will have to say that he does identify the two things. At this point, as Socrates hints, he already ceases to be the frank and vigorous opponent he promised to be. There are some things that even a Callicles will blush at; that being so, he begins to be vulnerable in much the same way as Polus was, though Plato does not choose to make a great deal of the point.

Socrates now embarks on a pair of arguments to undermine the identification of the good and the pleasant. These can be passed over; the first is extremely weak, while the second is only slightly less so (in effect, it accuses Callicles of inconsistency in calling intelligence and manliness good things, and then going on to identify good with pleasant. But if the 'identification' of good and pleasant is taken in the way I suggested, i.e. merely as the assertion that a thing was worth pursuing just in so far as it was pleasant, then clearly the inconsistency is no more than superficial. More specifically, the crucial move from 'the good are good through the presence of good things' to 'the good are good through the presence of pleasure' [498 d] is possible only because of Callicles' agreement to the proposition that 'intelligence and manliness are different from [pleasure and therefore] the good'; but again, provided we allow that Callicles does not strictly mean to *identify* good with pleasant, then we could easily suppose that intelligence and manliness were good in so far as they were means to pleasure). But the two arguments are enough to force Callicles into the outright admission that there are better and worse pleasures, though he says that that was what he really believed all along. Socrates does not take him to mean *morally* better and worse (as we might have expected from some of the things that were said earlier): good pleasures are interpreted as being those that have beneficial consequences, bad pleasures the reverse. Our pleasures, Callicles agrees, like everything else, should be determined by what is good for us (499 e–500 a). (This at any rate seems to be what Socrates means by the odd statement that 'we do everything, even pleasant things, for the sake of good things'.) But then how can rhetoric be the key to the good life, when – as Socrates suggested earlier – it has no concern with what is best, only with the procurement of pleasure itself? Callicles suggests that there are some orators who do speak with a view to people's best interests, and don't merely try to gratify their audiences (503 a). But Socrates immediately assumes that saying what is in people's best interests means saying the sorts of things that will improve their souls (which clearly no one does – unless, as we are told later, Socrates himself); and that in turn means speaking in such a way as to mould them 'to a certain shape', as other craftsmen do with their material, bringing order and system to them (503 e–504 a). Only when men's souls are in good condition will it be of any profit to them to have their desires fulfilled; just as it is only healthy people who are allowed by their doctors to indulge themselves. And since keeping people away from what they desire is punishing them, it follows that being punished, not unrestricted licence, is the better thing for the soul. 'I don't know what you mean, Socrates,' says Callicles; 'ask someone else.' Socrates proceeds to finish off the argument himself. He repeats the point that virtue consists in a certain order (in the soul as in everything else); and orderliness in the soul is the same as self-control. Therefore it is the self-controlled soul that is good (not the licentious one, as Callicles proposed), and self-control, so Socrates argues, implies the presence of the other virtues. 'So it necessarily follows, Callicles, that the self-controlled man, as we have shown, is a good man in the complete sense, since he is just and manly and pious; and that the good man does well and successfully whatever he does, and that the man who does well is blessed and happy, and the bad man, the man who does badly, is miserable – and this will be the man in the opposite condition to the self-controlled man, the licentious man, the man you were praising' (507 b–c). Socrates adds that such a man will be loved neither by man nor by god, because he will be incapable of doing or sharing anything with anyone else. 'Thus after all injustice is worse for the man who does it than for the man who suffers it, by just the same degree as it is more shameful; and the man who is going to be an orator of the right kind must then be just' (508 b–c).

Let us review what has been going on in this long argument. Socrates' initial purpose is to shake Callicles from his contention that pleasure is desirable without qualification. A life of scratching would be just plain absurd; a life devoted to sexual perversions would be morally bad; other pleasures would be bad in a straightforwardly prudential sense. It is on this last point that Socrates proceeds to build. If there are good and bad pleasures, then the ability to do what is actually best for people is going to be more valuable than the mere ability to please them (though it is not clear exactly why Callicles is expected to be concerned with *other* people's interests). Doing what is best for people means making their souls orderly (from the analogy of the other sciences); therefore being punished (having one's soul set in order) is better than not being punished, if one has done wrong. But an orderly soul is a self-controlled one, and since excellence (virtue)[2] is always associated with order, self-control is the excellence of soul. Now since the good man does everything successfully (because he has the excellence of soul), and the man who does everything successfully is blessed and happy, it follows that the good man will be happy, and the bad man (who lacks the requisite excellence) will be miserable.

There is clearly an important gap in this last part of the argument:

for how can Plato assume that it is the same excellence of soul that enables one both to live virtuously and to live successfully? But I shall have more to say about this passage in a moment. (What is probably the usual diagnosis of the argument attributes to Plato the gross mistake of passing illegitimately between the two senses of 'doing well' [the Greek phrase functions in pretty much the same way as the English]. But since his opponents – or at any rate Polus and Callicles – regard doing successfully as actually incompatible with doing virtuously, Plato could scarcely be unaware of the ambiguity of the phrase in ordinary language; and if he was aware of it, he could scarcely make an important argument pivot on it.)

In the remainder of the dialogue, Socrates presses home his advantage over Callicles. For the most part, he simply expands on what he has already said; but the dialogue culminates in an elaborate account of the judgement of the dead, which he claims to believe as true, though Callicles will think it just a story (523 a). Before the judges of the dead, Callicles will be as defenceless as he himself will be before the judges here.

The moral is perfectly clear: that true happiness lies in making both oneself and others better men, not in the narrow pursuit of advantage in the ordinary sense. Philosophy, and not rhetoric, provides the key to life, because only the first will give us the knowledge we need in order to live the good life – or if rhetoric is needed, then it is the sort of rhetoric that Socrates practises (*cf.* 521 d–e, where he is made to claim that he is perhaps the only true practitioner of the science of politics, because the speeches he makes are aimed at what is best for his audience). Much of this latter part of the dialogue, as of the earlier part, is familiar and Socratic; but several things are new. One, of course, is Socrates' unusual immodesty. A second, and rather more important, new element is the *political* emphasis of Socrates' speeches. Some of the things that the historical Socrates said may well have had political implications; but there is no evidence that he was seriously interested in political reform (unless, of course, the *Gorgias* itself counted as such). In the last part of the dialogue, Plato is, I think, beginning to formulate the concrete proposals we find in the *Republic*. At least, we find him arguing for the most basic of all the assumptions that underlie the later dialogue: that the central function of the statesman will be to provide for the moral education of the citizens, and that in order to do that he will require knowledge, which can only be provided by philosophy. Thirdly – and this is the point that concerns me most in the present context – much of the detailed reflection is new, particularly about the way in which virtue can be said to be beneficial to us, and vice harmful. In the conversation with Polus, Socrates merely argued that vice was harmful, without telling us how it was harmful. And, as I argued, this was a crucial omission, because it is by no means obviously absurd to hold the opposite view, that vice is highly beneficial. In the conversation with Callicles, the point is attacked in a direct and positive way.

There are perhaps three lines of argument that Plato employs, which I list in ascending order of importance. 1. The unjust will be punished after death. Socrates claims to believe this, but presents no reasons why we should believe it. (No one has yet succeeded in explaining precisely how we are supposed to take Plato's 'myths' – with which his 'account' at the end of the *Gorgias* can broadly be classified. One particular problem affecting the *Gorgias* passage is that Socrates is made to profess belief in the truth of his account, and yet includes in it an idea to which Plato certainly never subscribed, namely that what survives the body is a kind of soul-corpse, which can bear marks and be 'hung up' as an example in the prison of Hades. But maybe 'believing the account true' need not involve accepting the literal truth of everything in it; and in any case how *is* one to envisage the punishment of the dead?) 2. The unjust man will not be loved by either men or gods, because he will be incapable of sharing in anything with anyone else. This is by no means an insignificant point; but Plato makes practically nothing of it (not so in the *Republic*). 3. Thirdly, there is the argument at 506 c *ff.*, which connects successful living with having an ordered soul, and order in the soul with self-control. This argument comes from the same stable as the Socratic analogy between vice and disease, and in fact what underlies it is, I think, an attempt on Plato's part to reinforce that analogy (even though he appeals in 506 c *ff.* to what happens in *all* the sciences, not just to medicine). That attempt continues in the *Republic*, where we not only find a remarkably similar argument to the present one (at the end of Book I), but the conception of virtue as an ordering of the soul becomes what is probably the most important single thread in the whole dialogue. At the same time, Plato goes to some lengths to close the gap in the argument which I pointed out earlier.

One final point on the *Gorgias*. In the end, Callicles turns out to be as disappointing an opponent for Socrates as Polus was. But there is no need to accuse Plato of cheating, although Callicles certainly might have made a better case than he does. Maybe Plato is re-producing the position Callicles historically held (if there was such a person; though in fact we know nothing about him besides what we can gather from the *Gorgias*), maybe even a historical conversation; but on the whole this seems unlikely. I believe that, just as in the case of Polus, we are intended to generalize from Callicles' weaknesses. Polus, like most other people, just hasn't thought things out properly; but even someone who has gone deeper, like Callicles (so I take Plato to be saying), can eventually be brought round, provided that he can be made to listen. There are some things at which anyone whatever will baulk; and once some ordinary moral notion is uncovered, the rest quickly follows. Thus Callicles is really beaten from the moment he accuses Socrates of lowering the tone of the argument. If this is Plato's point, he is in one sense right: it *is* hard – much harder than it might seem – to put up a consistent intellectual defence of a life of immorality. It is not inevitable that another man would be caught out like Callicles; there might be someone who was completely unshockable. But it seems likely that he would find life rather uncomfortable. Plato's instinct seems right when he suggests that such a man would be without friends; in which case, the Calliclean claim that injustice leads to the maximization of pleasure begins to have a slightly hollow ring.

In any case, Plato is himself unwilling to let the debate rest there, for the reasons that I gave at the beginning of this chapter. In the *Republic*, which is the subject of my next chapter, the same questions are raised again, with a completely new audience.

Chapter notes

1. From this point on, 'Socrates' without qualification will always mean Plato's Socrates. The historical Socrates will always be referred to as 'the historical Socrates' or 'the real Socrates'.
2. The word in the Greek is *aretē*, which covers not only human virtue, but the excellence of anything that is good of its kind: so a Greek can talk about, for instance, a knife or a horse as having *aretē* as well as a man.

5 Plato's 'Republic'

The *Republic* is a long and complex work. For my purposes here, I shall divide it into five sections: 1. Book I, which bears a close resemblance to the *Gorgias* in both content and structure; 2. Books II–IV, in which Plato outlines an ideal state, and derives from it a definition of justice; 3. Books V–VII, dealing with the nature and education of the rulers of the ideal state; 4. Books VIII–IX, which describe the various inferior constitutions and the individual types that correspond with them, and reach a conclusion on the main question posed at the beginning of Book II, about whether it is justice or injustice that brings happiness; and finally 5. Book X, which generally serves to round off the work by providing qualifications and additions.

1. Book I

Book I is in many respects a unit in itself. The central aim of the discussion is the 'definition' of justice. Socrates considers various suggestions, rejects them, and ends by saying in familiar fashion that the conversation has got nowhere. An early dialogue would have ended there; as Socrates says at the beginning of Book II, 'having said that, I thought I had finished'. But in this case, two of Socrates' interlocutors – Plato's brothers, Glaucon and Adeimantus – are dissatisfied. Towards the end of the conversation in Book I, Socrates had passed on from the attempt to define justice to discuss Thrasymachus' contention that it was less profitable than injustice; and Thrasymachus had not been able to meet his arguments. But Glaucon and Adeimantus think that he has given up too easily, and their restatement of the case for injustice is the starting-point for the remainder of the *Republic*. Thus Book I in effect serves as the introduction to the *Republic* as a whole. It enables Plato to give a preliminary airing of both sides of the question; and I think it is also intended to justify a change of method. Book I fails to find a definition of justice; and it also fails – if we take into account the complaints of Glaucon and Adeimantus – to give an adequate defence of justice. The reason for its failure is that it is based on the Socratic elenchus, which is better suited to the purposes of criticism than to the development of positive views. Book I represents all that can be achieved by the elenchic method, which depends essentially on the examination of the views of others; in Books II–X Plato begins through Socrates to lay out his own detailed views, much as he did in the last part of the *Gorgias*.

The argument develops gently out of a conversation between Socrates and Cephalus, who implies a definition of justice as telling the truth (or perhaps keeping one's promises?) and paying one's debts to god and man (331 b–c). The defence of this definition is passed over to the much younger Polemarchus, who appeals to the authority of the poet Simonides. Socrates provides a counter-example: it would not be 'just' to return weapons, or always to tell the truth to a man who had gone mad (in this context, it is clear that the words *dikaios*, 'just', and *dikaiosunē*, 'justice' have a very wide meaning: 'right', 'right behaviour' would perhaps be a more natural rendering). So Polemarchus suggests that what Simonides really meant was that justice was doing good to one's friends and harm to one's enemies (332 a–b). This is what Plato regards as the *politician*'s definition of justice, whether implicit or explicit: 'I think it must belong to Periander or Perdiccas or Xerxes or the Theban Ismenias or some other wealthy man who thinks he has great power', says Socrates at 336 a (*cf.* also *Meno* 71 e, where Meno puts forward as the virtue of a man 'the ability to run the affairs of the city, and in running them to do good to one's friends, harm to one's enemies, and to prevent harm being done to oneself'). We are being prepared, I think, for the Thrasymachean definition, according to which justice is merely whatever happens to be in the interest of those in power (and can therefore be ignored in favour of injustice – for who would prefer someone else's advantage to one's own?).

Meanwhile, however, Socrates launches an attack on Polemarchus' revised definition. First, he manages to reach the conclusion that justice is only useful when it's a matter of keeping things safe, not when it's a matter of using them (because then we need different kinds of practitioners, e.g. draughts-players, builders, and so on) (333 d). Socrates' point here is, I think, that if it's a matter of doing good to one's friends, then there are plenty of areas where one's friends would find it more useful if one were something else rather than merely just. Next, he argues that if a skill qualifies a man to produce one result, it also qualifies him to produce the opposite result; *ergo*, the just man will be good at stealing things as well as keeping them safe; 'so it turns out, as it seems, that the just man is a kind of thief' (334 a). (The assumption, made in this and in the last argument, that justice is a skill, *technē*, is, I think, merely an extension of the Socratic equation of virtue and knowledge.) One might object that even if the just man *were* good at stealing things, he wouldn't do it, so that the final step in the argument does not work. But this scarcely matters, because in fact it follows directly from the definition that it will sometimes be just to steal – namely, when what you steal belongs to your enemy. But then, Socrates goes on, since it is unjust to harm those who have done you no injustice (334 d), your 'enemy' must be the unjust man, your 'friend' the just man (strictly speaking, it ought to be the man who is unjust or just *to you*). Finally, Socrates asks whether it is the part of a just man ever to harm anyone, even the unjust. He argues that it is not: harming a man means making him a worse man (i.e. worse with respect to human virtue, more unjust), just as harming a horse means making it a worse horse; and it is not a part of justice to produce injustice, any more than heat cools things, or dryness wets them.

Plato seems to be guilty in this last argument of a fairly gross fallacy: harming a horse may make it a worse horse, but harming a man does not necessarily make him a worse man. It could be said on Plato's behalf that he has a strong reason for arguing as he does, in so far as vice, in his view, is the only thing that can really harm a man. But this does not alter the fact that what he is supposed to be arguing is that the just man will not harm people in the ordinary sense. So far as the present argument goes, the just man could do what he liked with his enemies, so long as he didn't make them worse men – and by the previous argument, they're bad already. But it is clear that Plato does not want to say that. His position is that the just man will not harm anyone, in any sense; rather, it is his business to benefit his fellows – and in the proper sense, that is, by improving them. This is the ideal that Plato wishes to oppose to the narrow view put forward by Polemarchus.

Thrasymachus now intervenes. Plato's portrait of him, which is drawn with some care, is to say the least unsympathetic, although it may be quite accurate (there are no doubts about Thrasymachus' existence, as there were about Callicles'). His general position – though it has been the subject of much disagreement – is very similar to that of Callicles in the *Gorgias*. He begins by defining justice as 'what is to the advantage of the stronger' (338 c), 'the stronger' being whatever faction succeeds in establishing itself in power (339 a). It follows from this that justice is 'someone else's good' (343 c), namely what is good for those in power. Conversely, *injustice* means looking out for oneself, and much more profitable it is: 'injustice . . . rules over the truly simple and just; they do what is to the advantage of the unjust man, who is stronger than they, and make him happy by serving him, and themselves not at all' (*ibid.*) The unjust man does better in business dealings; pays fewer taxes; helps his friends and relations; and profits himself when in office. Thrasymachus adds that he means the man who is unjust on a large scale, i.e. the tyrant, not the burglar or the pickpocket. 'Thus, Socrates, when on a sufficient scale, injustice is something stronger, more a mark of a free man, more masterly than justice' (344 c: *cf.* Gorgias' similar equation of freedom with control of others). More generally, the unjust are wise and good (348 d): in other words, what is called injustice is in fact true virtue. Socrates' response to this last point is significant: 'this is more difficult, . . . and it's hard to know how to reply. For if you suggested that injustice was profitable, but agreed all the same that it was wickedness, or something shameful, as some others do, I would have something to say to you, because I could base myself on common assumptions' (348 e). This is, I think, a deliberate reference to the *Gorgias*. 'More profitable, but more shameful' was precisely what Polus said; and Callicles' real position turned out to be not so different. Thrasymachus, on the other hand, will not baulk at anything. (He is, perhaps, the 'more energetic' opponent that Socrates foresaw in *Gorgias* 509 a.)

Socrates first forces Thrasymachus to agree that by rulers he means skilful rulers, those who possess the art of ruling (because a man who didn't might direct his subjects to do things that were *not* to his advantage) (339 c–341 b). Now the other *technai* are all concerned not with their own advantage, but with what is to the advantage of whatever they are *technai* of (medicine, for example, is concerned not with what it can do for itself, but with what it can do for the patient). But the *technai* 'rule over', exercise control over, their subject-matter; therefore no art (science) seeks what is to the advantage of the stronger, but what is to the advantage of the weaker, or whatever is ruled by it (342 c).

Thrasymachus, however, makes a fight of it, by attacking Socrates' nalogy: the ruler is really like the shepherd, who fattens his sheep for his own benefit and that of his masters, not for their own. This seems, on the face of it, a fair reply; but Socrates does not agree. First, he points to the fact that people who take up public office always demand to be paid for it, which suggests that it is not something profitable in itself. Secondly, he tries to separate off a *technē* of making money, which is practised by all *technītai* over and above their own special *technē* (an elaborate way of saying that we get paid for doing a job; being paid isn't itself a part of the job) (346 a *ff.*). In principle, Thrasymachus could simply reply that the art that *his* rulers possess is actually a branch of the art of money-making; but this would be inconsistent with his earlier admission that they possessed the art of ruling. However, it is clear that Thrasymachus need not have made that admission; all that was required was that those in power should know what was to their advantage, not that they should possess the art of ruling in Socrates' sense.

By this stage, the narrow question about the definition of justice is very much in the background; the issue at stake is 'how life is to be lived – what manner of life is the most profitable' (344 e). This in turn is related – as it was in the *Gorgias* – to the question about how a state should be governed. Thrasymachus sees power as a means to personal profit; Socrates sees the ruler as the true shepherd, improving his human flock with respect to the appropriate virtue or excellence. But just what is the virtue of a man? Thrasymachus now claims that it is what is called injustice. In reply, Socrates produces what seems to me the weakest argument in the whole book, at the end of which he concludes (350 c) 'then the just man is wise and good and the unjust evil and ignorant' (the argument involves at least two major flaws: firstly, it trades heavily on the ambiguity of the phrase *pleon echein,* 'to outdo', 'to have more' of something; secondly, it allows Socrates to move from 'is like what it is' to 'is what it is like'). But the next argument, which is designed to show that injustice is a source of weakness (Thrasymachus had claimed at 344 c that it was 'something stronger than justice'), is rather better: if cooperation is to be possible in any group, there must be 'a certain element of justice' present (352 c); without it, disputes and disagreements would arise which would prevent joint action (351 e–351 a). The same, Socrates suggests, will be true in the case of the individual: injustice will make him incapable of action because he is feuding and not at one with himself; and he will also be his own enemy, and the enemy of the gods, as well as the enemy of the just. This last point looks forward to the later books, where it is explained in what sense the unjust man is 'at variance with himself'. For the moment, Socrates simply draws the general conclusion that 'the just are clearly wiser and better and more capable of action' than the unjust, and not the other way round, as Thrasymachus had claimed (352 b–d). It remains, he says, to show that the just are also more happy; though he adds that to his mind, this is already clear. So we embark on the final and most important argument, which begins at 352 d.

As I said at the end of the last chapter, the argument is very closely related to that at *Gorgias* 506 c *ff.* In fact, it is little more than a detailed working out of the earlier argument, but with the difference that it makes no use of the concept of *order*. That particular concept was necessary in the context of the *Gorgias* in order to establish the point that human virtue was justice, not injustice: virtue, so Socrates claimed, is always associated with order; and the ordered soul is the self-controlled one. But in the debate with Thrasymachus, that point has already been won – or at any rate Thrasymachus has been made to concede it. Briefly summarized, the *Republic* argument is this: everything has its own characteristic activity, and also its own peculiar virtue, which is what enables it to perform its activity well. The characteristic activities of soul are 'caring and ruling and deliberating and all such things', and also being alive (or *producing* life?); these activities can therefore only be performed well if soul possesses its peculiar virtue, which we agreed was justice. Therefore only the just man will live well (successfully), and living well is the same as being happy. Therefore the just man is happy, the unjust man miserable.

The least satisfactory aspect of this argument (apart from the addition to the list of activities of soul of being alive – which would seem to involve the conclusion that the just man was somehow *more alive* than the unjust man) is that it does not seem at all necessary to suppose that the just man will in fact be any better at 'caring, ruling and deliberating' (assuming that this means something like 'controlling one's life') than the unjust man, unless we already assume that just ends are more worth achieving than unjust ones; and that is precisely what the whole argument is supposed to be trying to establish. This is essentially the same complaint as I made against the *Gorgias* argument: there seems no obvious reason to follow Thrasymachus in agreeing so readily that the virtue that enables one to live successfully and the virtue that enables one to live justly are one and the same. But some such reason does begin to emerge in the course of the next eight books.

2. Books II-IV

There follows the request from Glaucon and Adeimantus for further arguments. Glaucon gives what he calls 'the common view' of the nature and origin of justice: that it is a compact not to harm or be harmed, drafted by the weak to protect themselves against the strong. Justice represents a compromise 'between the best of all, which is to do injustice and not be punished, and the worst of all, which is to suffer injustice without the power of retaliation' (359 a). He recounts the story of Gyges the Lydian and his magic ring, which made him invisible, and so enabled him to seduce the queen, kill the king, and take power for himself. Imagine two such rings, Glaucon says, one for the unjust, and one for the just: both would behave in exactly the same manner, because injustice is clearly more profitable than justice, provided that one can get away with it. Glaucon therefore demands that justice be shown to be more valuable than injustice *in itself*, apart from questions of reward and punishment. Adeimantus adds his weight to the argument. It is really the *appearance* of justice which matters, he says, if we judge by the way in which justice is praised. Again, justice and virtue are always said to be honourable things, but difficult to attain, while injustice and vice are easy, and much more profitable. It is also claimed that the gods can be bought: 'They say that even the gods have apportioned calamity and misery to many good men, and an opposite destiny to the wicked. And mendicant prophets go to rich men's doors and persuade them that they have a power committed to them by the gods of making an atonement for a man's own or his ancestor's sins by sacrifices or charms, with rejoicings and feasts; and they offer their services in harming an enemy, whether just or unjust, at a small cost; with magic arts and incantations binding heaven, as they say, to execute their will' (364 b–c). For this they can refer to the authority of Homer and Hesiod; they can also produce 'a host of books written by Musaeus and Orpheus . . . according to which they perform their ritual, and persuade not only individuals, but whole cities, that expiations and atonements for sin may be made by sacrifices and amusements, which fill a vacant hour and are effective so long as we live and after death; the latter sort they call initiations, and they redeem us from the pains of hell, but if we neglect them no one knows what awaits us' (364 e–365 a. This and the last two passages cited are in Jowett's translation). What should an intelligent young man infer from all this? Clearly, deceit will pay best; a man will be able to have the profits of injustice, and also the benefit of a reputation for justice. The danger of detection by one's fellow-men can be obviated by forming secret brotherhoods and learning rhetoric; and the gods, if they exist, and are interested in human affairs, can be propitiated with a little expense.

Socrates agrees with some hesitation to the two brothers' request, and to 'seek out what each of the two things is and what the truth is about their relative benefits' (368 c). He proposes to look for justice first as it appears in a state: 'what if we were to imagine a state in the process of creation, and saw justice and injustice coming into existence in it?' (369 a). Hopefully, the discovery of justice in the macrocosm of the state will give them the insights they need to identify it in the microcosm of the individual. Socrates begins the construction. At first, the composition of the state is dictated by man's needs: so there will have to be a farmer to provide food, a builder to build houses, and so on. It is agreed that the best arrangement will be for each man to do one job, among other things because different men are naturally fitted for different functions (370 a–b). Gradually the city expands, as different craftsmen are added; until at 371 e Socrates suggests that maybe he has enough. But then Glaucon insists that the citizens will need some luxuries. Socrates says that this will mean an unhealthy state; but since they are looking for injustice as well as justice, this is no matter. (Thus what Plato is constructing becomes at this point something less than an 'ideal' state; but later health is restored, with the account of education: *cf.* 399 e.) This means that we shall need many more inhabitants, and more land to put them on; we'll have to take some of our neighbours' territory, and if they're like us, they'll need some of ours too. The result will be war. So we will need soldiers to fight for us; and by the principle that each man is to be restricted to a single job, this must be a special class of citizens. The discussion now centres on these. We are told the qualities they will need; and at 376 c, Socrates launches into an account of how they will be educated, with the assurance that this will be relevant to the search for justice. His point is that education will produce justice; indeed, as it turns out, that is its most crucial function. The initial programme he lays out is made up of two parts: physical training, and the training of the mind through poetry and music. Plato's general view of education is of a kind of stamping of the character. If we are not careful, the lies and ugliness represented in the poets will rub off on our children; and music sinks particularly deep into the soul (401 d). (At 373 b–c, poets and musicians were introduced as belonging to the trappings of luxury, along with courtesans, cakes, and the eating of pork.) Only the most elevated and elevating poetry and music is therefore to be allowed into the city. The physical part of this early education is designed as a counterbalance to the effects of poetry and music: the latter tend to soften a man's disposition; physical training tends to harden it, by stimulating the 'spirited element' in him. The final aim of both parts of the educational programme is a harmonious combination of spiritedness and moderation or of courage and self-control (410 e). (This latter virtue is closely associated with the third of the four cardinal virtues, *wisdom*; so a little later, at 411 e– 412 a, the aim of education is said to be to fit together the spirited and philosophical elements in us [*cf.* also 375 b *ff.*]. The point will be of some importance in what follows.) The educator, Socrates sums up at 412 a, is a true musician, whose harmonies are of far greater value than those of the man whose business is with mere strings.

The next step is to decide who is to rule. Clearly, the older must rule the younger; and of the older, those who show the greatest concern for the welfare of the state. The term 'guardians', *phulakes*, is now to be used in the strict sense only of this highest class; the soldier class is to be called the *epikouroi*, 'auxiliaries' or, more literally, 'allies': their aim is to help the guardians proper 'to ensure that enemies from outside will not be able to injure the state, and to safeguard the bonds between the citizens, so that they will not wish to injure it' (414 b). So there are to be three classes: guardians, auxiliaries, and producers. In order to prevent the encroachment of one class on the functions of the others, Socrates proposes that the citizens of the state should be persuaded to believe in the fiction that god mixed different metals in the members of the three classes: gold in the first, silver in the second, iron and bronze in the third; that the state as it exists sprang fully armed from the earth; and that the oracle declared that it will fall when a man with bronze or iron in him becomes its guardian. This *gennaion pseudos*, or 'noble lie' (or, 'fiction': this is what *pseudos* is used to mean, for example, in 376 e *ff.*, in the discussion of literature), has occasioned much criticism; but it is no more than a mythical dressing-up (at least in the case of the first and third points) of things in which Plato literally believes. The only puzzling thing is that he asks that the guardians should believe in the story too; and yet they are – as we are shortly to discover – philosophers, lovers of wisdom and truth. In any case, the message is quite clear: the survival of the state depends on the strict separation of functions. That same point is re-emphasized in what follows. Socrates now makes the provision that the guardians and auxiliaries are to be fed and housed at public expense, and are not to be allowed to hold property of their own, in order to prevent them from being tempted by greed to turn on the other citizens. Greed and luxury, Socrates suggested earlier, are the main causes of all evils, both private and public (373 d–e; *cf.* 421 c *ff.*). But Adeimantus objects that to deprive the guardians of private property will be to deprive them of happiness. 'It would be no surprise to me,' Socrates replies, 'if this provision actually made them the happiest of all the citizens; but in any case our purpose in founding the state is not to make any single class outstandingly happy, but to provide for the happiness of the whole state' (420 b). If we make our rulers 'happy' in the material sense, we will make them anything except guardians. It is of no great importance if a potter stops being a potter; but if a guardian stops being a guardian, that spells the utter destruction of the state. Summed up, the aim is that 'each man should perform his own function and be one and not many, and hence that the whole city should be made one and not many' (i.e. by splitting up into partisan factions) (423 d).

There follow further remarks about education and legislation, until at 427 c–d, Socrates declares the state well and truly established. Where in it are we to find justice? If the city has been founded properly, it will be good; and it will therefore possess all the four cardinal virtues, wisdom, courage, self-control and justice. The state possesses wisdom in that it has wise guardians, courage in that it has brave soldiers (though there is a clear hint that there is some higher kind of courage than the one they possess: 430 c). Self-control causes more difficulty. 'It is a certain order,' Socrates says, 'and the control of certain pleasures and desires – as they say, the controlled man is "master of himself" ' (430 e). This implies to Socrates the existence in the human soul of two elements, one better, one worse; the worse element is 'numerically superior', and bad education and bad company can make it get out of hand. There is the same contrast between better and worse in the state: a multiplicity of all sorts of desires and pleasures can be found in women, slaves, and in so-called free men among the rabble; these stand in contrast with the few best, by nature and by education, whose desires and pleasures are few and moderate, and are 'directed by mind and true opinion'. Desires of the first kind are governed by the second kind, aided by wisdom, and it is by virtue of this that the state can be called self-controlled. More generally, self-control is described as 'the agreement between rulers and subjects about who should rule' (431 d–e). Earlier, self-control was described as consisting in two things in particular: 'being obedient to those in command, and being in command of oneself with respect to drink, sex and food'. The basic connection between the two things is that in both cases one set of desires is subordinated to another; but in the present context, Plato makes the connection much closer: the subordination of the lower classes to the highest is precisely in order to control their appetites, and so allow 'good sense' to prevail in the state as a whole.

So only justice itself is still left to find. Socrates proceeds to identify it with the basic principle that underlay the founding of the state: the principle 'that each man should be restricted just to that function for which his nature most fits him' (433 a). It is at first sight difficult to understand what this has to do with justice, in any conceivable sense. But the beginnings of an answer are, I think, suggested in the following speech of Socrates (433 b–c). 'It seems to me that what is left when you take away the three things we have considered, self-control and courage and wisdom, is what enables them to come into existence and preserves them . . . so long as it is present. And yet we said that if we were to find three of the four things we were looking for, what was left would be justice' (the reference is to 427 e–428 a. It is not clear exactly what the method is by which Plato claims to be working; but I propose to leave this problem to one side). If you possess the virtue of justice, Socrates seems to be saying, then you possess all the other virtues. This does indeed follow from the proposed definition: if the members of each class fulfil their proper functions, then the rulers will rule with wisdom; the soldiers will fight bravely; and the two lower classes will not try to usurp the functions of the highest. Now this suggests a clear connection between the definition and the sense which the Greek word *dikaiosunē* seems mostly to bear in the rest of the *Republic*: if *dikaiosunē* is the condition of wisdom, courage and self-control, then perhaps we should interpret it just as goodness in general, that disposition from which *all* right behaviour flows. At least, it is hard to see how 'justice' in any specific sense could plausibly be taken as the condition of the other virtues; though it must be admitted that Plato otherwise behaves as if he is defining a specific virtue, on a par with each of the others. (A further problem is that a list consisting merely of wisdom, courage and self-control does not look like an

C

exhaustive list of the virtues; in particular, we miss any direct reference to what would ordinarily be thought of as the central feature of *dikaiosunē*, namely that it has to do with the relations between citizens. But much the same problem will exist whatever our interpretation of the present passage. The gap is at least to some extent filled in the discussion of justice in the individual, when Socrates and Glaucon agree that the man who possesses the quality defined will not do the things normally considered unjust.)

Next, Socrates proceeds to try out his results, to see if they help us to discover justice in the individual – which they do. He argues that there must be the same traits in the individuals that compose the state as there are in the state itself; or in other words, that when we talk about the qualities of a state, we are really talking about the qualities of the individuals that compose it (435 e); and also that 'if two things are called the same, whether they are larger or smaller, they are alike in so far as they are called the same' (435 a). Thus the individuals in our state will be just, if the state is, and their justice ought to be the same. (In fact, the first of Socrates' two contentions here works well for wisdom, and courage; but it does not work for self-control, which exists in the state not because the individual citizens are themselves self-controlled, but because a certain relation exists between them.) If this is true, there ought to be three elements in the soul to correspond to the three classes in the state. This, Socrates suggests, is a difficult question; and indeed the whole inquiry that they are embarked upon cannot be properly dealt with by the present method. There is a longer way round, which we are told later (504 b) is the one that the guardians must follow. All the same, Socrates says, they will be able to reach conclusions that are no worse than their previous ones.

After detailed argument, the soul does indeed turn out to possess three parts, reason (*to logistikon*); the spirited part (*to thūmoeides*); and the appetitive part (*to epithūmētikon*). (In fact, Plato mostly talks about 'three things', or 'three kinds of thing', and only towards the end uses the word 'part'.) The individual, then, will be just in the same way as the state was: and this means each of the three parts or elements of his soul performing their own proper functions. The function of the highest part is to rule, that of the spirited part to be 'the subject and ally' of reason (441 e); and the two of them together, when properly educated, will set themselves over the lowest part. A man is wise if his highest part is in the right condition; courageous, if this is true of the spirited part; and self-controlled, if both the two lower parts are controlled by the highest. 'But then he will be just by virtue of the principle we have enumerated several times, and in that way' (442 d). Finally, Socrates proceeds to test his definition by reference to the 'vulgar' notions of justice: the man who is as we have described, as a result of his nature and education, will not steal deposits, loot temples, commit adultery, or neglect his parents. The 'vulgarity', as Socrates explains at 443 c *ff.*, lies in talking about justice in terms of a man's action, instead of his internal condition: the criterion of justice is not so much what he does, as what his soul is like. The kind of definition we ourselves would probably expect would be precisely an account of types of *behaviour*; and this is the main reason why Plato's definition seems so peculiar. What he is after, as the last passage shows, is what we mean when we call a *soul* just, what the possession of the virtue called justice does to a soul. And what it does is to allow it to function as it should. Injustice, Socrates says at 444 b, is a kind of factional dissent between the three parts of the soul, 'an uprising against the whole soul of a part of it, which aims at power when it is not fitted for it, but is by nature the natural slave of [the highest part], whose noble descent fits it not for slavery, but for rule'. Next, he draws the parallel between justice and health, injustice and disease: healthy things produce health, unhealthy things disease; similarly, just things (actions) produce justice, unjust things injustice. Again, producing health in the body means making its elements (i.e. the 'humours') stand in the natural relation to each other, while disease is the reverse; and the production of justice and injustice involves the same ordering of parts. Hence, Socrates concludes at 444 d–e that 'virtue will be a kind of health and beauty and well-being of the soul, and vice is a kind of disease and ugliness and weakness'. He then puts the crucial question, about whether it is more profitable to do just and virtuous things, which lead to the acquisition of justice, or to do unjust things and so be unjust – without reference, of course, to material rewards or punishments. Glaucon replies that the question is absurd; if life can be made unendurable by disease, how much more intolerable it must be when the soul, 'that very thing which gives us life', is corrupted (445 a–b).

The core of Plato's argument in all this is that justice and virtue represent the natural state of the soul. The old analogy between vice and disease implies this, of course, by itself. But in the present context, the idea is developed in much greater detail than before. Plato's basic position is that the rational part is by nature supreme, and that if it is allowed to function uninterrupted, then we will always follow the path that reason tells us is best (which is orderly, rule-governed behaviour). But the two lower parts, and especially the lowest, can get out of hand; and if they do, we lose sight of our goal. This is the origin of vice. (Some are less well endowed with reason, and are thus less well able to resist the incursions of 'pleasures and desires'; hence the necessity for the establishment of the guardians: see 590 c *ff.*) This is a not unattractive position. After all, we do like to think of ourselves as rational creatures; and it is often, though not always, desirable to think before we act. What still remains to be established is that there is only one kind of life compatible with rationality; that is, the virtuous life that Plato wants to recommend. (Why not, for example, a perfectly rational and systematic pursuit of *bad* ends?) In the following books we find Plato providing at least some kind of basis for this assumption.

3. Books V–VII

At the end of Book IV, Socrates proposes to examine the inferior kinds of state, and the characteristics of soul that go with them. But he is compelled instead to give a full acount of the way in which women and children are to be treated in the ideal state. These and other assorted topics take up the bulk of Book V. Then at 473 c–d, Socrates explains the one essential change that has to take place if his state is to stand any chance of becoming a reality (though he makes it clear that any actual state may well do no more than approximate to the ideal). The suggestion is made with the greatest hesitation: 'either philosophers must become kings in the cities, or the people who are now called kings and rulers become philosophers'. Glaucon says that people will scoff at such an idea; and Socrates proceeds to mount a defence.

The defence rests on the theory of forms, which is introduced here for the first time in the dialogue. Beauty and ugliness, he suggests, are both single things; 'and the same with justice and injustice and goodness and badness and every kind of thing – each is in itself just one thing, but because they appear everywhere in combination with actions and material things and each other, each of them seems to be many things'. Now ordinary people are concerned only with these things in their multiple aspect; with the many particular beautiful things, for example, not with 'beauty itself' (*auto to kalon*), which is what occupies the attention of the philosopher. In virtue of this, the philosopher is said to possess knowledge, while the state of mind of the ordinary man is no more than opinion (476 a–d). There follows a difficult and probably confused argument to support the last point. For my purposes here, the most interesting part is at 478 e *ff.*, where Socrates begins to draw his conclusions: any one particular beautiful thing, he says, will always appear ugly too (i.e. at some time, in some relation, from some direction, or to some people: cf. *Symposium* 211 a); and similarly with just things, holy things, things that are double, large, small, light, heavy – everything is at once what we say it is, and the opposite of that (479 b). Thus, the man who is restricted to objects of this kind can only have an imperfect understanding of what beauty, justice, or anything else really is; unlike the philosopher, who 'sees' these things in themselves. Or in other words, the philosopher possesses *knowledge* about beauty, the other man merely has *opinion* (so, at least, Plato puts it). But clearly, Socrates continues at the beginning of Book VI, the best guardians of the laws and institutions of states will be those who possess knowledge, and who therefore have a 'clear standard' in their souls, to which they can refer, like artists, as they lay down whatever laws are necessary about what is beautiful, just and good (484 b–d). (I have cut many corners in this account; but I believe that it reproduces Plato's basic meaning. The main difficulty in the argument is caused by the fact that it hinges on the notorious verb *einai*, which is roughly translated as 'to be', but whose actual range of meaning is much wider. It is worth adding that the passage as a whole is one of the most hotly debated in the whole of Plato.)

The philosopher, then, has insight into 'beauty itself', 'justice itself'. But what kinds of things are these? The information given here is scanty, though it is to some extent filled out later on in Book VI, and in Book VII. They do not 'wander about because of coming-into-being and decay' (485 b), unlike particular beautiful and just things, but always remain exactly what they are. Actions and things 'combine' with them, or 'share in' them; they also mix with each other in things (i.e., as we are told, beautiful things are also ugly, and so on), but are in themselves quite distinct and separate. Given this description, as far as it goes, there seems little difficulty in identifying the 'forms' of beauty and justice as *universals*, and the beauty and justice of particular things as their instances. But as the sequel shows, this is only a part of Plato's meaning.

Socrates next shows that the philosopher will possess all the virtues, simply because of the nature of his activity. He will be truthful, because he is a lover of wisdom; self-controlled, because his desires are channelled towards knowledge; and so on. (A full description of the philosopher's virtues would, I think, link them specifically with his *knowledge*. But as yet the content of that knowledge has not been explained.) But Adeimantus objects that as things are, philosophers are not like that at all: those who study philosophy are either useless, or 'altogether odd – not to say objectionable' (487 d). Socrates explains: the true philosopher seems useless simply because no one recognizes the value of his knowledge; people think that anyone and everyone is qualified to take a hand in running the state – just as if sailors decided that there was really no need for studying navigation. And the corruption of the philosophic nature is all too easy in a democratic society. The real corruptors are not a few individual sophists, as one might think, but the people at large: they sit together and shout their approbation or disapproval, always too loudly, and eventually a young man's head is turned, so that he thinks as they think, and is as they are (492 a–c). The sophists, Socrates adds, only teach the opinions of the masses, and dignify it with the title of wisdom. They are like keepers learning to manage a large and powerful animal, by studying its likes and dislikes: good is what pleases it, bad what displeases it. The masses, we are told, have utterly no conception of goodness and beauty, and are unfitted to judge anything – hence their low opinion of philosophers (493 a–d). (At 499 d *ff.*, Plato uses a slightly gentler tone.) Still, a very few of the best natures will survive; and the hope is that they will coincide with the sort of state we have been describing.

Socrates turns to discuss the higher education of the rulers, which will turn them into true philosophers. They will travel the longer way round that Plato talked about earlier, and reach a more complete understanding of the virtues (504 a–d). But this can be acquired only by first grasping a still higher object of study: the form of the good. A man will be a poor guardian of the just and the beautiful (or fine), if he does not know how they are *good* (506 a).

This is obviously very closely related to the ideas of the historical Socrates. He too insisted on the need for full knowledge; and for him too, full knowledge meant not merely knowing what was right, but knowing that this was best for one. But he never dreamed of the complex metaphysical structure with which these ideas are now connected.

'Every soul pursues [the good] and does everything for the sake of it, having some instinctive conception of its existence' (or, 'that it is something'), 'but . . . not being able to grasp sufficiently *what* it is, or to reach a stable opinion about it in the way that it can about the other things' (505 d–e). It is not pleasure, as the ordinary man supposes, because there are bad pleasures (a point which recalls the argument of the *Gorgias*); nor is it knowledge, as the more sophisticated would have it, for if they are asked what it is knowledge of, they can only reply 'of the good'. Socrates comes under pressure to say what *he* thinks the good is; but he says that in the context of the present discussion (which, as we were told before, is not at the highest level) he cannot talk directly about the nature of the good; the best he can do is to talk about 'one of its offspring, the one most like it' (506 e). There follows the first of three difficult similes. The 'offspring' of the good is the sun: just as this makes the objects of sight visible, and is responsible for coming-into-being and growth, so the good makes the objects of thought knowable, and is also the cause of 'their being and their essence' (or, 'their being and what they are', 509 b) ' – not being itself [their?] essence, but being still above and beyond essence in dignity and power' (in the same way as the sun causes coming-into-being without *being* coming-into-being). What Plato is suggesting, then, is a hierarchy of forms, with the form of the good at the top. Two reasons are given for its hegemony: firstly, that it is what makes the other forms knowable; secondly, that it is the 'cause of their being and essence'. The first of these two ideas is perhaps easy enough to grasp: it is a close relation of the old point that moral knowledge includes knowledge about our best interests. Here, though, the idea is extended beyond moral knowledge: the form of the good gives knowability to *all* the forms – and, as we learn later, 'we are accustomed to posit a single form for each group of things to which we apply the same name' (596 a). It is at any rate clear how the form of the good is relevant to the physical world and (therefore, *a fortiori*, to the forms of physical objects and qualities). According to the *Phaedo* (96 a *ff.*), the most important single principle to be assumed in the explanation of the physical world is that *everything in it is for the best*. And this perhaps may begin to explain what Plato means by the perplexing statement that the form of the good is 'the cause of the being and essence' of the other forms. If the structure of the world is determined by what is for the best, then the good must also be a formative principle in the world of forms, which the physical world mirrors (the second most common metaphor for the relation between forms and particulars, after that of 'sharing in' – used in the passage where the forms were introduced in Book V

– is that of 'copying', 'imitation': particular things are copies of the forms, though always inferior ones). And one can perhaps go one step further: what for Plato typically separates the good from the bad is the general idea that the good is something *ordered and harmonious* (a notion that has been especially prominent in the *Republic*). It may be, then, that he identifies the operation of the good just with the presence of order and harmony in things: whether in the human soul and human behaviour, in the heavens, or in the objects of mathematics (for which, see below). But the the information we are given is too scanty to be certain of Plato's meaning.

Socrates passes on to another illustration, which is an extension of the first (509 c). We are to imagine a line divided into two unequal parts, the longer part corresponding to the intelligible world, the shorter to the visible world. Next, we are to divide both parts again into two, in the same proportion. The first and shorter part of the lower section is to correspond to 'images', i.e. shadows and reflections cast by the sun, the second to actual objects, natural or artificial. In respect of 'truth', Plato says, these two groups stand to each other in the same relation as the objects of opinion and knowledge (510 a). In the lower part of the upper section, 'the soul uses the things copied in the lower section as images and is forced to make its inquiries from hypotheses, not travelling to a beginning [principle] but to an end [conclusion]; in the other part – which concerns the path to an unhypothetical beginning – it goes from a hypothesis and without the images used in the part below, proceeding only by means of the forms themselves' (510 b). Socrates explains that what he is referring to in connection with the lower of these two parts is the mathematical sciences, which use visible diagrams (the 'images' that are talked about), but are not really talking about these, but about forms: the form of square, the form of diameter, and so on. Finally, we have the ascent to the 'unhypothetical principle' (i.e., presumably, the form of the good), from which the soul is said to descend again without using any sensible object, and beginning and ending with forms (511 b–c).

This passage is even more difficult than the one preceding it (I have suppressed some of the more problematic parts in my summary). But the main point that Plato is attempting to make seems to be about the various degrees of 'clarity' to be gained from the different kinds of object or method. When we turn from shadows to the objects that cast them, we think we are grasping things as they really are (see 510 a). But these objects can in their turn be used merely as the 'images' of still higher ones; and full insight can in fact only be gained when they are left behind altogether, and the soul operates with the forms alone. In the first simile we are told about the relation of the form of the good to the other forms; here we are told about how the world of forms stands to the physical world, and how knowledge of the one stands to 'knowledge' of the other.

It is by now quite obvious that it is insufficient to regard Plato's forms merely as universals; for on the face of it universals seem to be less, not more, substantial than their instances. Further, if there are systematic connections between universals, this seems to be because such connections exist between their instances, and not *vice versa*. (Yet at the same time, as we saw earlier, the identification of forms with universals is justified by at least a some of the things that Plato says about them.)

In the third and final simile, Socrates describes the progress of the philosopher to full knowledge. Men are pictured as being tied up in an underground cave, in such a way that they cannot look round. Behind them is a path leading up to the daylight; between them and the path is a fire, and between them and the fire is a wall, along the top of which artificial objects and figures of men and animals are carried in a continuous puppet-show. The only things the prisoners can see are shadows on the cave wall in front of them – their own, and those of the puppets; and they take them to be the real thing. Then we are asked to imagine one of the prisoners being released: first he is shown the puppets, then the fire; naturally, he is blinded, and tries to get away, back to the shadows, thinking them really to be much clearer than what he is being shown now; then he is dragged forcibly up into the sunlight, where he is at first unable to see anything at all; but as he gets used to the light, he begins to be able to see shadows and reflections, then the things that cast them; from here he goes on to look at the sky at night; and then finally he is able to look upon the sun itself, and 'realizes that it is this that provides the seasons and the years and governs everything in the visible world, and is in a certain way responsible for all the things that [he and his fellow-prisoners] saw' (516 b–c). Now, Socrates suggests, the man would do anything rather than go back to living in the cave; but if he did go back, the others would laugh at him because he would be unable to see in the unaccustomed darkness, and would be unable to compete with them in judging the shadows. The cave, of course, represents the visible world, the fire in it the sun; the path upwards is the ascent of the soul into the intelligible world. 'God knows if the image is a true one. But this is how it seems to me. The form of the good is the last thing to be seen in the world of knowledge, and can only be seen with effort. But once it is seen, then the realization follows that this is what is responsible for all things that are right and beautiful, having given birth to light in the visible world and what provides it [i.e. the sun], and in the intelligible world itself providing truth and understanding. It is only the man who sees this [i.e. the form of the good] who can act wisely in either private or public life' (517 b–c). (One special problem of interpretation deserves comment here. Plato seems to suggest that people fail to see things directly even on the level of the visible world; and this, on the face of it, is both odd and unnecessary. The reasons for it may be that he is thinking specifically about human conceptions of *virtue*. The puppets, perhaps, represent virtue as it can be exemplified in human society – that is, in Plato's state, which is to be drawn according to standards provided by the intelligible world; the shadows are ordinary conceptions of virtue, which are as it were two-dimensional copies of true human justice.)

Socrates draws on his simile to suggest that education is not a matter of planting knowledge into the soul, but of 'turning its eye in the right direction' (518 b–d). Wisdom is unlike the other virtues in that it seems not to be acquired by habituation and practice, but to be a permanent possession of the soul, which can be turned either to good or to bad use (518 d–519 a). Our rulers, of course, will have followed the upward path. But there is a problem: philosophy is a supremely pleasant activity; how then are we to get our philosophers to come down again, and give humanity at large the benefit of their vision of the good? They will be told that they are bound to serve the state in recompense for the upbringing and education they have received from it; and that in any case they are better qualified to rule than the others (520 a *ff.*). (The latter point recalls a passage in Book I [347 b *ff.*], where it was argued that better men will consent to rule for fear of being ruled by those inferior to themselves.) There follows an account of the studies the philosopher will follow before his final ascent to the good. These are generally characterized as studies which will 'draw him away from what comes into being towards what is' (521 d). Unsurprisingly, they turn out to be the mathematical sciences of arithmetic, plane geometry, solid geometry, astronomy and harmonics. None of these sciences studies physical things in themselves, even the latter two: properly understood, their concern is with ideal movements, ideal harmonies – and these can never be found in the physical world. It is absurd, Socrates suggests, to suppose that celestial phenomena are not liable to deviation, when they are bodily and visible (530 b). If perceptible movements and harmonies are of any use at all, it is in that they can suggest theoretical problems for the scientist. Pursued in any other way, Socrates suggests, the sciences in question will not fulfil their proper purpose which is to help in the search for 'the beautiful and good' (531 c). But he insists that they are only preliminary to the highest study of all, that of dialectic. Glaucon asks for an account of this, but Socrates says that he would no longer be able to follow. What he does tell us about dialectic, and about the superiority of its methods over those of mathematics, is little more than we knew already from the illustration of the divided line – and that little is perhaps even more perplexing. Nor are we told anything more about the form of the good, the chief object of the dialectician's study; only that he must be able to define it, 'having abstracted it from everything else'.

This is tantalizing. It seems likely that the description of the philosopher's ascent to the good is the description of a project rather than of something already systematically achieved. But the crucial point that concerns me is that without any fuller account of the philosopher's final vision, we still have no concrete reason for sharing Plato's optimism that unhindered operation of reason would necessarily lead us to choose the virtuous life; in which case, the argument that he mounted at the end of Book IV remains fatally flawed. But more arguments are to follow.

4. Books VIII–IX

In Book VIII, Socrates resumes the topic which was left hanging at the end of IV: the four inferior types of constitution (or 'diseases of the state', as he calls them at 544 c), and the characteristics of soul that go with them. Once this topic is completed, he says, they will have 'unmixed' justice set side by side with 'unmixed' injustice, and will then be able to judge the one against the other, as they originally intended. Socrates, in mock-epic style, represents the four other states as stages in an inevitable decline from the best state, or 'aristocracy': though it will be difficult to destroy our state, still 'nothing that came into being can escape destruction' (546 a). First in the decline comes the Spartan or Cretan type of constitution 'which is praised by most people' (544 c). This type lies somewhere between aristocracy and oligarchy, sharing features of both; but the most prominent characteristic is the rivalry and contentiousness that arises because of the domination of the spirited element in the individual citizens (548 c). Next comes oligarchy, in which the poor are ruled by the rich. The rot set in under the 'timocracy', which made the mistake of allowing private wealth; now the size of one's purse outweighs all other considerations. This has all sorts of undesirable consequences: party strife between rich and poor; inefficiency, dispossession, crime. In the corresponding individual the two higher parts of the soul are enslaved by 'the appetitive and money-loving element': 'reason is only allowed to think about how to convert less money into more, the spirited element is allowed only to admire and honour wealth' (553 d). Stinginess, and the desire to keep his good reputation, restrains the man's worst desires; but still he has them: just watch him, Socrates says, when he becomes the guardian of an orphan, or has some other opportunity to act dishonestly. So he, like the oligarchic state, is 'not one but two'; but on the whole his better desires (comparatively speaking) control his worse ones (554 d–e). The next change is from oligarchy to democracy: the uncontrolled pursuit of wealth by a few leads to the creation of a large class of dispossessed people, which eventually realizes its strength and takes power. The distinguishing feature of democracy is that anyone and everyone can be a citizen and have a share in governing; for the most part, offices are distributed by lot (557 a). (This is what Plato finds least acceptable about democracy. At least 'timocracies' and oligarchies make *some* attempt to separate the sheep from the goats.) The state is anarchic in an easy-going sort of way; the freedom everyone boasts about is the freedom to do just as one likes. The corresponding character comes into being in a corresponding way: the 'necessary' desires of the oligarchic man are displaced by 'unnecessary' ones (i.e. those which are not either indispensable for the continuation of life, or beneficial in some way, 558 d–e). These latter are pictured as redefining all the virtues – much as Callicles and Thrasymachus had done: arrogance is breeding, anarchy freedom, waste magnificence, shamelessness the sign of a real man (560 e–561 a). But when the democratic man gets older, if he is lucky, he will sober up a little, and allow some of the exiled desires to return; he achieves some kind of balance, honouring all desires equally, and ruled by whichever desire happens to be strongest at the time – whether to get drunk, or to drink nothing at all; to do a bit of training, or just to do nothing; even to play at philosophy (561 c–d). Finally, there is tyranny. Under a democracy, the poor despoil the rich (who are for the most part the more orderly element by nature, 564 e); there is renewed party feuding; then someone comes forward as 'champion of the people', and to begin with, that is what he is; but eventually, by gradual stages, he turns into a tyrant. Socrates describes his rule: at first, he is everyone's friend; but soon he has to devise ways of keeping people occupied, which makes him unpopular; he has to get rid of all the best men; he has to free slaves or hire foreigners for his bodyguard, so that having got rid of the best sort of people, he has to live with the worst. He's also a temple-robber and parricide: having exhausted the temple-treasures, he turns to killing and robbing the rabble that spawned him. Thus in trying to escape the frying-pan (or, as Plato actually says, the smoke) of the slavery of free men, they fall into the fire of the tyranny of slaves (i.e. of the tyrant's slave bodyguards).

At the beginning of Book IX, Socrates turns to examine the individual characteristics that correspond to the tyrannical state. There are, he suggests, certain violent and brutish desires in all of us. Among the rest of us (even among those who seem to be altogether admirable people) they only 'peer out' in our dreams; but the tyrannical man is completely ruled by them, even when awake (576 b). People like this either go off and become mercenaries, or if there is no war they stay at home and turn to crime; but the man who has in him 'the greatest and most powerful tyrant' himself becomes tyrant (575 c–d). He associates only with flatterers, and if he needs anything from anybody, he is quite ready to cringe on his own account. He is never anybody's friend, always either master or slave, and knows nothing about true freedom or friendship (575 e–576 a). He is also the supreme representative of injustice, if the original definition of justice was right (i.e. because his soul is most out of joint). Socrates sets out to establish formally that he is also the least happy. In the first argument he makes use once again of the analogy between state and individual: the tyrannical individual is like the tyrannical state, and so on; therefore, if one state is happier and more virtuous than another, the same must be true of the corresponding individuals (576 c). The tyrannical state is certainly the worst and the least happy; so, therefore, is the corresponding individual (the point being, of course, that his vice and his misery are directly related). Socrates works this out in detail: in the tyrannical state the best elements are enslaved; this kind of state therefore does what it wants least of any state (i.e. because it does not do what is best for it, and it must want what is best). Similarly, the corresponding soul has its best parts enslaved, and it too fails to do what it wants, 'that is, if we speak about the soul as a whole; stung by the gadfly of desire, and always dragged forcibly about, it will be full of confusion and remorse' (577 e). Again, the state is always in penury; the tyrannical soul, similarly, is always 'in need and unsatisfied' (577 e–578 a. The analogy here becomes somewhat forced: if it is the tyrant who is 'in penury', then he is being compared with himself; if it's the people at large, then the best elements in the state are being compared with the worst in the individual, since it's clearly his *desires* which are being described as unsatisfied; and if the reference is to both together, then we have both problems at once). Both state and individual will also be full of fear; and just as the state will be 'fuller than any other of lamentation and groaning and mourning and grief', so too will the individual soul, 'driven mad by desires and passions' (578 a). It was these considerations that made Glaucon agree that the tyrannical state was the most wretched of all; we must therefore draw the same conclusion about the corresponding individual (578 b).

The general construction of this argument leaves a good deal to be desired (if two things are alike in some respects, it does not follow that they will also be alike in others – and in any case the tyrannical state and the tyrannical individual are miserable in different ways: the state is miserable because each of its members is miserable, but the individual soul is not miserable because its parts are). But there is one important new development in it. In addition to the familiar – and essentially abstract – argument that the unjust man will be unhappy because he is not ruled by reason, and therefore does not act for the best, Plato suggests that he will be unhappy because his condition is *disagreeable*: he will feel remorse; he will suffer anguish because his desires are insatiable (if this is Plato's meaning); and he will be in a state of continuous fear. The first of these three points scarcely carries any real conviction; it is, I think, little more than a deduction from the view Plato holds of the nature of the human soul (reason is by nature good; if it goes wrong, it is because it has been 'enslaved' by lower desires. But in that case, so Plato seems to be supposing, it will still put up a struggle). But the other two points are more plausible; they are enough, at any rate, to undermine the idea that the mere freedom to do what one wants guarantees one's happiness.

That, Socrates says, is our first argument. (All five types are arranged in order of their degrees of happiness – which is, of course, the order in which they were introduced.) The second argument envisages a dispute between the representatives of three different kinds of life about which of their lives is the most pleasant. The three are the philosopher, the lover of honour, and the man who spends his life in the pursuit of profit. Each represents the domination of a different part of the soul: in the first, reason dominates; in the second, the spirited part; in the third, the appetitive part. (This gives us the connection with the argument about injustice. The unjust man is the man in whom one of the two lower parts is in control; the question then is whether his pleasures are greater than those of the just man, in whom reason rules.) All three will praise their own lives; but the prize, Socrates says, must be given to the philosopher, on two grounds: firstly, that he alone has experience of all three different kinds of pleasures; secondly, that only he possesses the capacity to reason, which is the instrument of judgement (580 d–583 a). (If a philosopher suddenly decided he preferred a different kind of life, I suppose Plato would take this as evidence that he was not a true philosopher, and had not tasted of the true joys of knowledge; and given that the objects of his knowledge are supposed to be the good and the beautiful, this may look a fairly reasonable position. A similar justification could be given of Plato's second consideration. But without the theory of forms, neither point would amount to very much: even professional philosophers might actually prefer watching football; and if they did, no amount of reasoning with them would help. Much the same points also apply to the third argument, which is closely related to the present one.) In the third argument, the dispute is decided in a rather more complex way. Firstly, it is agreed that there is a state intermediate between pleasure and pain which is actually neutral, but *seems* pleasant in contrast with antecedent pains. For example, sick people will say that the most pleasant thing in the world is to be healthy; but when they *were* healthy, no such thing would have occurred to them. Pleasure cannot be the mere cessation of pain, because there are some pleasures – e.g. the pleasure of smell – which have no antecedent pains. Still, many pleasures are simply the relief from pain: e.g. most of the pleasures of the body (or, as Plato calls them, 'the so-called pleasures that stretch through the body to the soul') (584 c). Having thus shown that people can be mistaken about pleasures, and how they can be mistaken about them, Socrates proceeds to apply the point to the types of pleasure presently under consideration. Both the pleasures of the philosopher and those associated with the lowest part of the soul are a kind of 'filling-up': in the one case the soul is filled with understanding, in the other the body is filled with food and drink. (The third type of pleasures, those associated with the spirited part, are more difficult to fit into this scheme, and are introduced only at the very end of the argument [586 c–d]. But clearly Plato would like to regard them in the same way: they are described as 'the satisfaction (literally, 'filling-up') of anger and of [the desire for] honour and victory'.) But food and drink are less substantial than knowledge; in which case the filling-up in the case of the bodily pleasures is less of a filling-up than in the case of the pleasures of the philosopher; the latter are therefore more real than the former. Most people don't realize this, because 'they have no experience of wisdom and virtue', and therefore know nothing of real pleasures; like cattle, they keep their heads firmly down, and are satisfied with fattening themselves and copulating, fighting each other to get more – they're insatiable, 'because what they fill up is insubstantial and holds nothing, and what they fill it up with is equally insubstantial' (586 a–b). Finally, Socrates adds that if the lower two parts of the soul are to achieve 'the truest pleasures of which they are capable', they must follow the dictates of reason (586 d–e). (These 'truest pleasures' are perhaps those whose concomitant pains are the least severe; i.e. the pleasures of moderate indulgence.)

Justice, then, is more pleasant than injustice. (Perfect justice, as Socrates half-jokingly calculates, is exactly 729 times more pleasant than perfect injustice.) Book IX ends with a vivid illustration of the effects of justice and injustice on the soul, which is intended as a kind of summary of results. We are asked first to imagine a monstrous creature with many heads, some of them the heads of tame animals, some those of wild ones; the creature can sprout or change all these at will. This, of course, represents the appetitive part of the soul. The spirited part is somewhat smaller, and has the shape of a lion; the rational part, which is in the shape of a man, is smaller still. All three are somehow fused together, and contained in a single shell, so that from the outside the whole looks like a single human being (588 b–e). Anyone who maintains that injustice is more profitable than justice is maintaining that we should strengthen the monster and the lion in us, and leave the man to their mercy. The supporter of justice, on the other hand, says that we must rather strengthen the man; we must make an alliance with the lion and watch over the monster like an expert farmer, encouraging the tame elements and cutting back the wild ones; the general aim being to promote harmony among the disparate trio, not dissension. And, says Socrates, it's the supporter of justice who is telling the truth. Virtue must be a matter of subordinating the beast to the man (and not *vice versa*, as would be involved in Thrasymachus' identification of virtue with injustice); and this is also inevitably the most profitable course – profitable, that is, in the true sense. Reason must rule in everything; where a man's best part is weak by nature – as with manual workers – and cannot rule the beast in himself, he must be the slave of the man who does have the divine ruling element in him; not for the benefit of the ruler, but simply because it is better for everyone to be ruled by reason: if a man has no such ruling principle in himself, one must be set over him from outside (590 c–d). (This last point thus effectively disarms the highly emotive word 'slave': if anyone is a slave in the state, everyone is.)

The argument that is implied in this whole passage is that reason is what distinguishes man from the beasts, and makes him superior to them; to allow oneself to be dominated by passion is to obliterate that distinction. Rationality, then, as Plato argued at the end of Book IV, is man's natural state. And we meet once again with the same problem as before: the fact that man is by nature a rational creature does not in itself entail that he is also virtuous by nature. For that, we need the successful completion of the project announced in Books VI and VII – or else it has to be shown that injustice is undesirable in terms of its external consequences, a task which is undertaken in Book X. (Since the project to find the good is not in fact completed, either in the *Republic* or anywhere else, it is fair to say that Plato fails to make his case that injustice is something undesirable in itself. Aristotle says that the project is actually impossible, because the form of the good does not exist.)

5. Book X

The first half of Book X is occupied with further discussion of the position of art in the best state. Then, at 608 c, Socrates remarks abruptly that 'we have not yet gone through the greatest rewards and prizes of virtue'. He begins his account with the preliminary point that the soul is immortal (a proof is given). The just man will be loved by the gods; everything will therefore happen for him in the best way possible, 'unless it is necessary for him to suffer some evil for wrongs done before' (i.e. in a previous existence: as we learn from the myth at the end of the dialogue, souls are caught in a continuous cycle of death and rebirth). 'This then must be our conception about the just man, whether he is in poverty, or is ill, or suffers any of the other things that people think of as evils; namely, that these things will end in some good for him, whether in life, or even in death. For the gods never neglect anyone who is serious in his desire to become just, and who tries by practising virtue to be as like a god as it is possible for a man to be' (612 e–613 b). The reverse will be true of the unjust man. The just will also mostly have a good reputation among their fellow-men; and in general they have all the rewards that Glaucon originally gave to the unjust, at the beginning of Book II: they have power in their own cities, if they want it; they can marry anyone they like; they can have their pick of sons-in-law. The unjust, on the other hand, 'though they may escape at first, are mostly found out in the end; they become objects of ridicule, and when they reach their miserable old age, they are trampled by everyone, foreigner or citizen'; finally they are bound, whipped, racked, have their eyes burnt out, and are impaled on a stake (613 b–e). But, Socrates says, these rewards and punishments will be nothing compared with those that await the just and the unjust after death. These are described in the 'myth', told by one Er, who miraculously revived while lying on his funeral pyre. There is much else in this elaborate story, but most of it is of no particular importance to my present purposes. At the end, Socrates draws the moral that 'we should practise justice with wisdom, in order that we may be at one with ourselves' (i.e. each with himself, and also with his fellow-citizens) 'and with the gods' (621 c; *cf*. 351 d–352 b). In a sense, this summarizes the whole of the *Republic*. Internal harmony is the intrinsic reward that justice brings; harmony with one's fellows and the favour of the gods are what Plato regards as the two greatest of its external rewards. If we are just, then, as Socrates announces in his last two words, 'we will do well'.

I hope that I have done enough to show where I think the strengths and weaknesses of Plato's case lie. (The strongest part of it is the point that is presupposed by the whole argument of the *Republic*, that justice is a necessary precondition of friendship and social harmony. Whether or not his political proposals are the right way to go about achieving either is another matter.) Here, I wish to pick up two problems which were left hanging from the chapter on the *Gorgias*. They arose out of the fact that Plato's arguments about virtue and justice consisted entirely in an attempt to show that they were *good for the individual*: this seemed, on the face of it, to imply that Plato excluded the possibility that a man could do something simply because it was right, which looked an odd position for a moralist; secondly, it seemed to imply the absence from his scheme of any notion of *altruistic* behaviour.

The first point can be dealt with fairly easily. When Plato argues that it is good for me in some way to do a particular thing, he does not necessarily mean that this should be my immediate *motive* for doing it. Clearly I can act rightly without knowing at all that what I am doing is good for me. And in fact this will be precisely the situation of nearly everyone in Plato's state – everyone, that is, except the philosophers. One might even describe Plato's aim as being to explain why rightness is a motive for action, in reply to those who reject it in favour of another. Further, even if virtue is justified in terms of what is good for the individual, we must not forget that Plato seems to go on to justify *that* by appealing to the nature of the world as a whole (the desirability of virtuous behaviour is justified by reference to the fact that it creates and preserves a harmonious soul; the desirability of having a harmonious soul is justified – at least in the first instance – by reference to the harmony of the universe at large).

Given the point that Plato is not suggesting that people's motives should always be self-centred, then there will also be room for altruistic action in Plato's scheme – at least in principle. Altruistic action is action done from altruistic motives; and it remains altruistic whether or not it also happens to benefit my soul. But does Plato in fact acknowledge the existence of such a thing? Certainly the philosopher-kings will give up both their pleasures (i.e. the pleasures of philosophy) and their material interests in order to rule for the benefit of their subjects; but it is significant that although they are supremely virtuous, they will still apparently need to be compelled to take office. It is true that they will be given reasons, one of which is that it is *just* that they should serve the state; but the case is not argued on the basis that they have a general obligation to serve their fellow-citizens, but on an appeal to the idea of reciprocity (more specifically, perhaps, to the analogy of one's duty to one's parents: service is owed in payment for one's upbringing and education). On the other hand, the members of the soldier-class will evidently be quite ready to sacrifice their lives for their fellows. Our conclusion, I think, should be not that there is no room for 'altruistic benevolence' in Plato's system, but that the role it plays is very small. (In Aristotle, as we shall see, its role may be smaller still.)

6   Plato's 'Statesman' and 'Laws'

The *Statesman* can plausibly be seen in many respects as a preface to
the *Laws*, intended to explain and justify its methods. One of the
central points in the dialogue is about the essential limitation of
written law. By its very nature, Plato says, law is general, and can
never prescribe what is best and most just for everybody without
exception; 'for the dissimilarities between human beings and their
actions, and the complete absence of any kind of stability in human
affairs make it impossible for any art at all to lay down rules in any
sphere which will hold in an unqualified way about everything'
(294 b). This crucial statement has implications far beyond those
that Plato himself draws out in the immediate context. He spoke in
the *Republic* as if the really difficult part of the philosopher's task was
the climb up to the form of the good; the only problem then was how
to persuade him to come back to the cave to apply his knowledge.
But now, I think, he has recognized that the matter of the application
of the philosopher's knowledge brings its own special difficulties;
for if law suffers from being too general, then the same must be even
more true of the philosopher's knowledge, since good laws will
themselves already be an attempt to apply his insights. Even in the
Republic, Plato had said that the philosopher will need *experience* in
addition to his knowledge, and had made provisions by which he
could acquire it (that is, by spending fifteen years before the final
stage of his education in military commands or junior civilian offices:
539 e–540 a). But, as I have suggested, there is no sign that Plato
there saw the full complexity of the phenomena with which political
science (I mean, of course, in the ancient sense) has to deal. The
insight of the *Statesman* has two important consequences. Firstly,
Plato is much less certain of the possibility even of approximating
to what he considers the ideal system of government, i.e. government
by those qualified to govern, the exponents of political science (or,
as the *Statesman* mostly calls it, the 'science of kingship', *basilikē
technē*). The *Statesman* seems in the end to recognize that we will have

to settle for a second-best kind of state; and the state constructed in the *Laws* is for the most part precisely of that kind. The second consequence of Plato's new realism is that he turns (in the *Laws*) to a much more detailed examination of the type of legislation needed to achieve his end – which is, as in the *Republic*, the creation of a virtuous and well-ordered community.

Thus far, I have assumed that the theory of forms we find in the *Republic* (or something like it) survives into the late dialogues. It must be admitted, though, that this is a matter of some disagreement among scholars. The key exhibit in the dispute is the *Parmenides,* in which we find Plato himself (in the guise of Parmenides) subjecting the theory to serious and apparently well-directed criticism; but there is evidence too on the other side. For my purposes here, it will be enough to mention briefly the main internal evidence provided by the *Statesman* and the *Laws*. The *Laws* makes no explicit reference to the forms; on the other hand, the members of the nocturnal council, the highest officers in the state, will be expected to involve themselves in detailed studies, at least one of the aims of which is the discovery of 'the common element in all the four virtues, the thing which is one and the same in courage and self-control and justice and wisdom, and which we therefore say can justly be called by the single name "virtue" ' (965 d). This does not, on the face of it, differ very much from some of the concerns of the philosopher-king in the *Republic*. In the *Statesman,* the knowledge of the statesman is still evidently to be thought of as independent of, and prior to, his experience of things in the physical world; and the method that is employed throughout a major part of the dialogue seems to involve a similar assumption (see below). In general, there is enough to make it reasonable to suppose that the metaphysical structure of the *Republic* has by no means been completely abandoned. But, as I have suggested, it has now been pushed rather into the background, at least so far as concerns ethics and politics.

The *Statesman*

The *Statesman* is not one of Plato's most attractive works; indeed large parts of it are downright tedious (as Plato himself acknowledges). (The main speaker is a guest from Elea, the home town of Parmenides, although Socrates is also present. In the *Laws* he is nowhere to be seen.) The purpose of the conversation is to define the statesman, or the art of statesmanship – more generally, it is to help us to be better philosophers (285 d); but that part of it is of no concern to us here. The definition is achieved by means of the method of 'division', on which Plato seems to have hung much hope in the latter part of his life. The method, briefly, is as follows: first, a broad genus is selected under which the thing being defined seems to fall, and this is then divided according to species (or, according to *Phaedrus* 265 e, 'according to its natural articulations'); then the relevant subdivision is divided, and so on until, hopefully, the definiendum is reached, and the definition can be read off. Here, the first attempt of the Eleatic stranger to define statesmanship ends in failure. The definition has made the statesman a kind of herdsman or shepherd; but this, the stranger says, is wrong, because while a herdsman is responsible for every aspect of the welfare of his charges, a statesman is not – some human needs are looked after by merchants, some by farmers, and so on. The reason for their failure (which will, I suppose, be instructive for the dialectician) is illustrated in a myth. There are, we are told, two recurring stages in cosmic history: in one, god controls the world and imparts its rotation to it directly; in the second, released from divine control, 'fate and innate desire' (272 e) turn it back on itself, so that it rotates in the opposite direction. We ourselves live in the second era, in which chaos will gradually increase. In the divine era, on the other hand, the age of Kronos, life was – perhaps – perfect. There was no war; there were no political constitutions; because everything happened in reverse, men sprang up automatically out of the ground, and there was no need for taking wives and having children; fruit grew in abundance without cultivation. Whether or not life was in fact perfect depends on whether people then made good use of their opportunities: whether they spent their time in search of knowledge, or whether they frittered it away in eating and drinking and chatter (272 b–d).

Our mistake, the stranger says, was to make the statesman too like the divine shepherd of the age of Kronos; he is not a god, but a man. Only a god could be a shepherd of his human flock, in the true meaning of the word (274 e–275 a). It is probably also part of Plato's intention to emphasize the limitation of the capacities of the human statesman (*cf.* 275 b–c), and the intractability of the material with which he has to work – a world which has an 'innate desire' to return to disorder and primeval chaos.

Two modifications are made to the definition: the statesman (or king) is now said to have 'concern for' his subjects (i.e. a more general term than before) rather than to look after them like a shepherd; and in order to distinguish him from the tyrant, it is added that his subjects must willingly accept his rule. But the stranger is still not satisfied. After a methodological account of the employment of examples, he uses one to show where we have gone wrong, and how we can improve things. What we have still failed to do is to separate statesmanship adequately from other functions in the state (just as if we defined weaving as 'the art which produces woollen protections against the weather' [280 e], without noticing that there are many other arts that contribute to this end).

There follows another methodological digression, which is of more than incidental interest (283 b *ff.*). The pedantic nature of much of the conversation leads the stranger to distinguish between two kinds of 'excess and deficiency': first, the straightforward kind, where one thing is larger or smaller than another; and, second, where a thing exceeds or falls short of the right measure. This second kind is found especially in the sphere of *actions*: a good action is essentially one that achieves the right measure, a bad action one that fails to do so. But the same principle is also crucial to all the sciences: for 'it is by preserving due measure that they achieve goodness and beauty in their products' (284 b). Plato himself does not seem to have made any great use of this distinction (though there is a cryptic suggestion at 284 d that it will be needed for some purpose in the future); but as we will see, it is later taken over by Aristotle, who uses it as the basis of one of the central doctrines of the *Ethics*, the so-called 'doctrine of the mean'.

At this point, the digression for a short while takes on a rather more general tone. People miss this kind of distinction, the stranger says, 'because they are not accustomed to dividing things by classes' (285 a: the Greek uses the word *eidos*, which is one of the two main words for 'form'; but it would probably be wrong to introduce that technical sense here); or, in other words, because they are not trained in dialectic, of which the present dialogue is an example. There follow some brief remarks about the methods and aims of dialectic. The general picture that is given of it is of a kind of mapping process, a plotting of the relationships between different kinds of things (we have just had one concrete example, in the distinction between two kinds of measurement). Now this raises a problem. If the map-maker wants to know what to insert in a particular segment of his map, he can go and see what is there on the ground; but the dialectician, as Plato himself complains, cannot always do this

(285 d–286 b: in the case of lower objects, there are 'perceptible likenesses' to which he can point; not so in the case of the 'finest and most important' objects). And statesmanship itself seems to be a case in point; for, as we will find, Plato wants to distinguish the 'true' statesman from all actual statesmen. Where, then, does he get his privileged knowledge about statesmanship from? The answer to this problem is, I think, provided by the *Republic*. In the argument with Thrasymachus in Book I, Socrates reached substantive conclusions about statesmanship by considering what a science is: no science, he said, seeks its own interest, but the interest of whatever is in its charge; the same must therefore be true of the science of statesmanship. The *Statesman* itself makes *science* the starting-point of its divisions; and although there is no trace of the particular argument used in the *Republic* (since the disinterestedness of the statesman is assumed from the beginning), it makes very good sense to suppose that some such approach underlies Plato's procedure. When he defines statesmanship he does not think of himself as constructing an ideal, but rather as understanding something about how things are. (There is obviously much in common between this and the picture of dialectic given in *Republic* Books VI–VII; but the question about the development of Plato's views in this area is, as I have suggested, a very complex one.)

After the digression, the stranger proceeds to make the necessary separation of the statesman from other categories in the state: first, from the producers; second, from slaves, labourers, and businessmen; third, from heralds, official clerks, soothsayers and priests; and, fourth, from actual statesmen, the rulers of existing states. These, we are told, are the arch-illusionists, the worst of the sophists (291 c, 303 b–c); and the constitutions under which they rule are also counterfeit. There are five types of these: kingship, tyranny, aristocracy, oligarchy, and democracy, which are distinguished from one another by whether one man rules, or few, or many, or by whether the rich or the poor rule, or whether rule is carried on by force or by consent, or whether with a code of laws, or without one; in none do we find the mark of the true constitution, which is that it is ruled by *science*. There will be only a few men who are capable of acquiring the science of kingship; but what decides whether they are rulers and statesmen is whether or not they possess this science, not whether they are few or many, rich or poor, whether they rule by force or by consent, with a code of laws or without one. (At 292 e–293 a, the important proviso is made that a statesman need not himself be in power; he may simply be an *adviser* to a ruler [see also 259 a]. A number of members of the Academy did in fact serve in this capacity in various royal courts, a practice in which they were most notably followed by the Stoics. Plato's own ill-fated adventures in Syracuse probably belong in the same category.) Once again, Plato uses the ubiquitous analogy with medicine: we do not judge a doctor by whether he works according to fixed rules, or by his pocket, but by whether he looks after us in a scientific way. All this seems acceptable to the stranger's respondent (a young namesake of Socrates), except for the idea that a king may rule *without law*. There follows the passage I quoted at the beginning of this chapter, in which the stranger explains the limitations of written law. The legislator, like the athletic trainer, makes his prescription for people as a whole, and thus 'will never be able to give each single individual exactly what is right for him' (294 e–295 a). Even the true statesman may need to make use of laws; but if he does, he will not treat them as unalterable, if he discovers ways in which they can be improved. He may go against the written law, he may even use force; the only thing that matters is that he does what is *beneficial* (296 d–e). This, the stranger says, is the only correct kind of constitution. A second-best type is the constitution that keeps to its laws with absolute rigidity; worst of all is the constitution in which the laws are overridden for private motives – for the sake of profit, perhaps, or the giving of personal favours. This is quite different from the modification of law by the exponent of the science of kingship. The laws under the inferior constitutions may not be ideal, but they are at any rate the fruit of experience, and have the consent of the people. Anyone who breaks them does far more harm than the laws themselves may do because of their rigidity. The stranger now gives us a final list of seven types of constitutions (301 a *ff.*): the best type, and three pairs of 'imitative' types, consisting in each case of a 'law-abiding' constitution and one that flouts laws: monarchy and tyranny, aristocracy and oligarchy, and two types of democracy. These inferior constitutions arise, we are told, because people have despaired of finding anyone worthy of kingly power; though if one such man were to appear, he would be welcomed with open arms. 'But since as things are . . . a king is not born in cities like the king bee in the hive – a single individual immediately superior both in body and in soul – men have to get together and write laws, so it seems, following as hard as they can on the tracks of the truest constitution' (301 d–e).

At 303 d, we return for the last time to the problem of the definition of the statesman. Having distinguished him from existing rulers – who are said to be, not statesmen, but *stasiastikoi*, 'party men' – the stranger finally separates him from orators, generals and judges. All three types have a role to play in the state, even the orators (we have come a long way since the *Gorgias*). The function of oratory will be to 'persuade the mass of the people, by telling them stories [*dia mūthologias*] rather than by teaching' (304 c–d). Statesmanship is distinguished from oratory as the science that controls it, in that it decides when and how it should be used; similarly with generalship. Lastly the judge is separated off on the grounds that he does not himself make laws, but merely applies them. Statesmanship, then, is 'the science that controls all these sciences, and takes care of the laws and everything in the city, and weaves everything together in the most correct way' (305 e).

In the very last part of the dialogue, Plato explains his metaphor of 'weaving together'. We begin with what the stranger says is a dangerous point, one that the disputatious are likely to seize on with delight: that in a certain way the two virtues of courage and self-control are opposed. The reason for saying this is that the qualities associated with these two virtues never seem to be appropriate in the same situations. We approve of gentleness and quietness, and also of a certain sharpness and vigorousness; but where we require the latter, people who show the former qualities are called cowardly and sluggish; where we require the former, sharp and vigorous becomes aggressive and unbalanced. This 'enmity' between the two virtues carries over into their possessors: the two types, the courageous and the self-controlled (or, more strictly, 'those who tend more towards courage', 'those who tend more towards the orderly', 309 b), are always at odds with one another. The statesman's task will be to weave them together (after having killed, banished or thoroughly disgraced those who cannot share in virtue, but 'are driven by their evil nature into godlessness and violence and injustice', and having made slaves of 'those who grovel in ignorant subservience', 308 e–309 a), and he will use two methods: intermarriage, and the implanting in them of right opinion about 'the beautiful, the just and the good' (309 c).

There is little trace of this theory of types in the *Laws*, which, like the *Republic* (410 c–e), simply emphasizes the need for combining the two qualities in individuals. The most significant point made in this passage of the *Statesman* is that a quality is not necessarily praiseworthy in itself; it may be appropriate in some situations, and totally inappropriate in others. This is further evidence of Plato's increased awareness of the complexity of the subject matter of 'political science'.

The *Laws*

The *Laws* is the longest of all the dialogues (and in this short chapter only some three books are treated in any detail). It was probably also the last written; and there are signs of hurriedness in both style and construction. But for all that it is a fascinating work. In it, Plato lays down a detailed legal framework for an imaginary Cretan colony, to be called Magnesia. The choice of Crete is deliberate: the Cretans, along with the Spartans, were generally held to have the best type of constitution (*Rep.* 544 c, *Laws* 631 b; *cf. Laws* 712 e). Even so, Plato thinks this type of constitution far from perfect; and he begins the whole work with a detailed criticism of it.

The three partners in the conversation are an unnamed Athenian, who takes the lead; Cleinias, a Cretan; and Megillus, a Spartan. The Athenian's criticism of the Cretan and Spartan constitutions is that they aim at producing the single virtue of courage, which is in fact only the fourth of the cardinal virtues (630 c–d, 631 c–d). This preoccupation with martial qualities is admitted by both the others (they could scarcely do otherwise); Cleinias, for example, supports the view that every city is in a perpetual state of war with every other (625 e). But gradually the Athenian brings them to see the importance of the other virtues – and especially that of self-control. Self-control, *sōphrosunē*, is perhaps the most important of the virtues in the *Laws* as a whole, although it is officially placed only second in 631 c–d, after wisdom. 'When people inquire into legislation', Plato roundly declares at 636 d, 'the inquiry is almost wholly about pleasures and pains.' (This remark may be supposed to cover courage, as well as self-control, if courage can be defined as the ability to resist the fear of pain [*cf.* 646 e *ff.*]; and perhaps other virtues too. But as the surrounding context shows, it is self-control that is at the front of Plato's mind.) The Athenian suggests that one way of training men in self-control would be to institute properly regulated drinking-parties, in which men would learn to resist pleasures by being exposed to them, in the same way as they acquire courage by being exposed to fears. In the middle of this discussion there is a short but interesting treatment of the general purposes of education (643 a *ff.*). Not unexpectedly, these are summed up as the production of virtues:

' "Education" means education from childhood towards virtue, making a man desire passionately to become a perfect citizen, who knows how to rule and be ruled with justice' (643 e). A man is envisaged as a battle-ground of opposing forces: he has two 'foolish advisers', pleasure and pain (foolish, because they judge everything simply by themselves, without reference to good and bad); there are also opinions about the future, i.e. fear, the expectation of pain, and confidence, the expectation of good (in a closely similar passage in the *Timaeus* [69 c–d], it is the 'opinions about the future' which are said to be the advisers; and this is, I think, what Plato really intends here); opposed to these is the golden rope of calculation, that is, calculation about good and bad. In the state, this element is *law* (which will, of course, include laws about education); this provides the necessary assistance to the 'gold in us' and helps us to overcome the other elements in us (644 b *ff.*). (Interestingly, the *Timaeus* passage also mentions *anger, thūmos*; and the whole analysis is related, in the sequel, to the tripartite theory of soul. It may be that we should assume a similar background to the present passage; but we should also beware of making Plato more rigid than he really is.) The emotions are themselves imagined as being strings, pulling us this way and that: we are the puppets of the gods, constructed 'either as their plaything, or for some serious purpose' (644 d). This low estimate of the value of human activities is a recurring motif in the *Laws*.

At the beginning of Book II, Plato continues his general discussion of education. 'I maintain', the Athenian says, 'that a child's first sensation is of pleasure and pain; and that these constitute the field in which virtue and vice first attach themselves to the soul; as for wisdom and true opinions, it is a fortunate man who acquires these even as he approaches old age . . . Education, then, I call the first acquisition of virtue by children' (653 a–b). What education does is to inculcate the right habits in us; only later will we grasp the reason *why* they are right. Something like this idea was present in the *Republic*: after all, the soldier-class were *habituated* to virtue, and only later acquired truly philosophical virtue. But here the wisdom that brings the perfection of virtue is not the wisdom of the philosopher, but *true opinion*, precisely the stage that the philosopher leaves behind. Further, habituation is now an integral part of the process of the acquisition of virtue, rather than being an inferior substitute for it. All this has at least two implications: first, that virtue is open to all; and, second, that the doctrine 'virtue is knowledge' will apparently have either to be abandoned, or at any rate to be thoroughly modified (I shall come back to this point at a later stage).

Next, the stranger turns to the role of art in education. The criterion of excellence in art is whether it gives pleasure – not to anyone, but to 'the best, those who have been properly educated' (658 e). If we follow this criterion, art will be properly educative, part of the process that 'draws children towards the principle that the law declares to be right, and has been endorsed as such by the oldest and best among us, by virtue of their experience' (659 d). The most important requirement to be laid upon the artist is that he should always stress the indispensability of virtue for happiness. So-called goods – health, beauty, wealth – are only in fact good for the just man; for the unjust man they are evils (*sc.* because they increase his potential for vicious behaviour). Cleinias is unconvinced, so the Athenian mounts an argument to persuade him (662 b *ff.*). He proposes that if justice is worth having, it must be something pleasant, because 'no one would willingly do something that would not bring him more pleasure than pain' (663 b); but it is in fact pleasant: it brings 'fame and praise from men and gods'; it also means that we do not injure others, and are not injured by them (663 a). (There is also a slightly puzzling subsidiary argument in 663 b *ff.*, which I shall pass over.) But finally, even if it were not true that justice brought pleasure, it would still be beneficial to pretend that it was; i.e., presumably, it would be beneficial to the state at large (663 d).

According to the *Laws*, the universal goal is pleasure; according to the *Republic*, it was the good. In one way, the change is unimportant, because even in the *Laws* the (really) pleasant is the same as what is (really) good. At the same time, it is a further indication of a relaxation of the narrow intellectualism of the *Republic*. Virtue is not now a matter of *suppressing* the desires, but of persuading them to cooperate, to desire 'the right pleasures at the right time and in the right amount' (636 d–e). It is in this sense that we are to understand the passage at 644 b *ff.*, where Plato talked about the 'victory' of the golden element in us. In the *Republic*, the victory of the rational part meant substituting its own desires and pleasures for those of the appetitive part; in the *Laws*, since *all* desires now belong to the irrational part, this view is no longer possible.

With the end of Book II, we also reach the end of Plato's account of moral education. Much of the rest of the *Laws* (Books III–XII) is of rather less importance for my present concerns; and accordingly

I shall concentrate on a few crucial passages, and merely summarize the rest.

Book III discusses various different past and existing states, in an attempt to discover the reasons for their success or failure; Book IV turns directly to the setting up of Magnesia. At 712 b–c, the Athenian asks what constitution it will have. It is hinted that it will be most like the Cretan and Spartan constitutions, which turn out to be impossible to classify; and for the good reason that all the main types under which constitutions are classified 'are not constitutions at all, but are simply ways of running cities by enslaving some parts of them to others' (712 e–713 a) – a vice that, with all their checks and balances, the Cretan and Spartan constitutions avoid. It will be ruled by law, but not by law that favours any one group at the expense of the whole city. Similarly, no one will be appointed to office for any other reason than that he excels at obeying the established laws.

The constitution of Magnesia in fact turns out to be a modified version of the 'best state' of the *Statesman*. The main change is that the function of improving the law is given over, not to a single outstanding individual, but to a committee, the so-called 'nocturnal council' (this is introduced only at the very end of the *Laws*). The other central features of the constitution, which is painstakingly worked out in the following books, are these. The whole citizen body is to receive the same education, and is to be eligible for office (hence the suggestion that was made at 643 e, that the aim of education is to produce perfect citizens, who 'know how to rule and be ruled'), even for membership of the nocturnal council; only the higher an office is, the more stringent the mechanisms to ensure that it is filled by the right people. The nocturnal council in a certain sense corresponds to the guardian class of the *Republic*; but there is nothing to correspond to the auxiliaries, for now all citizens are liable to military service. This seems at first sight to entail the abandonment of the principle that each man should stick to a single function; but this is not in fact the case. All the citizens are – ideally – gentlemen farmers; no citizen, Plato says, nor even any slave belonging to a citizen, is to take up any of the productive arts; 'the skill of a citizen, which requires a great deal of practice and study, is the establishment and preservation of the order of the community, which is not something that can be done on the side. Virtually no human being is capable of following two callings or trades efficiently, or even of following one himself and supervising someone else in another' (846 d–e). Granted, the same man will sometimes have to combine military service with the holding of office; but the same was true in the *Republic* (that is, in the case of junior offices). The trades and professions are all to be put in the hands of aliens, who are to be strictly regulated (and even they must stick to a single job). The land is to be held inalienably by 5040 citizen families. The ideal, Plato says, would be that all property should be held in common; but we must remember that we are talking about men, not gods (739 d–e). (In the *Republic*, too, he had suggested that we could probably only hope for an approximation to the ideal.) A further concession to reality is that although land-holdings will be equal, holding of wealth will not: some of the colonists who come in will be richer, some poorer; and so to avoid trouble and dissension, four permanent property-classes are to be established, to ensure that offices, taxes and distributions are made according to worth. A man's worth, Plato roundly declares, is measured not only by his personal virtue and that of his forebears, his physical strength and good looks, but by his 'use of wealth or by his poverty' (744 b–c). (This seems in open contradiction to the principle enunciated earlier, that the sole criterion for the distribution of offices should be obedience to the laws. What probably accounts for it is an assumption that we find implied in the *Republic* [564 e]: 'if everyone is engaged in making money', Plato says there, '*those who are the most orderly by nature for the most part become wealthiest*'. Exactly the same tension is found in Aristotle.) But there are to be very strict rules to prevent the acquisition of wealth beyond a certain point; exceptional wealth, Plato establishes, is incompatible with exceptional virtue (742 e *ff.*).

After first having raised the question about the constitution of Magnesia, the Athenian turns to the question of legislation (718 a *ff.*). Each law will consist of two parts: an introduction, which will be aimed at persuading the citizens to behave in the right fashion; and the law proper, which lays down more or less precise rules, and the penalty for disobeying them. Book V begins with a general introduction to the legal code as a whole, in which we find some familiar themes: the importance of setting the correct value on one's soul (726 a *ff.*); the idea that vice fills a man's soul with 'evils and remorse' (727 c); that the worst penalty of vice is that it cuts one off from the company of good men; and so on. (There is also a striking reminiscence of the agnosticism of the *Apology* about life after death [727 c–d]. But there is a problem about how these introductions are to be taken: sometimes their content seems to be dictated more by its usefulness than its literal truth. The problem is the same as that of the interpretation of Plato's myths, to which the introductions are closely related – they are the products of the orator of the *Statesman*, who works *dia mūthologias*.) But the two most interesting sections come at the end. First there is a short passage about the necessity for avoiding excessive love of self. The striking thing is that we are not told to love others instead; what we must do is to admire others as much as ourselves, and look for people better than we are. There is, in Plato, not much room for personal affection; what interests us in other people is their *virtue* (731 d *ff.*). (Later, in Book VIII, two acceptable kinds of 'friendship' are described: one between two virtuous equals, and male homosexual love that aims at the improvement of the younger party [837 a *ff.*]. This is, I think, the nearest Plato ever gets to including benevolence among the virtues. (Then, after a short passage which talks about the necessity for avoiding excesses of joy or grief (as so often in the *Laws*, it is the *middle way* that has to be followed), there is an official account of the relation between virtue and happiness. Once again, the argument is wholly in terms of pleasure and pain: everyone desires a life in which there is a predominance of pleasure over pain; and this is the life of virtue (as anyone who knows it will tell you); in the licentious life it is the other way round. But what the pains of the licentious life are we are not told; we are left merely with a suggestive comparison of the moderation of the pleasures and pains of the self-controlled life with those of the licentious life; and a disingenuous juxtaposition of the healthy and the unhealthy life. As a justification, it is, to say the least, skimpy; but then conformity is a much more important virtue in Magnesia than a demand for reasons.

In the second half of Book V and in the following books (VI–VIII) the city is established: its administration is set up, rules are laid down for marriage and procreation, education, sex, agriculture, and trade. Then, in Book IX, there is an account of criminal law, in the middle of which Plato launches into a discussion of the theory of punishment. On his view, the purpose of punishment is not retribution, but the reform of the criminal (there is also a question of recompensing the victim, but that is a separate matter). This view is based on the Socratic paradox that all vice is involuntary; which Plato now defends (860 c *ff.*). There are essentially two kinds of injury: firstly, injury that is done by accident, or under compulsion; and secondly, injury that is done for neither of these reasons. Both types are involuntary; if the second is called voluntary, it is so only in contrast with the first. Injustice of the second type (which is the only type properly called injustice) always stems from one of three causes: anger, pleasure, or ignorance. Anger and desire can 'compel' us to do things (i.e. when we know we shouldn't, or at least have right opinions); and if we do them out of ignorance, then obviously we can't help it. (We will find Aristotle subjecting this analysis to some judicious criticisms.) Thus one of the two Socratic paradoxes is retained; but the other, the identification of virtue with knowledge, seems finally abandoned.

Book X is a reasoned rejection of atheism, which is associated with materialism, and with the immoralist position (for this last point, see especially 890 a). Plato sets out to prove three things: 'that the gods exist, that they are good, and that they value justice more highly than men do' (887 b). It is the gods, for Plato, who provide the final justification of law. Thus at the beginning of the whole work, Zeus and Apollo are said to have been responsible for the establishment of the laws of Crete and Sparta (and it is not, I think, felt as a contradiction when it is later said that they were laid down by Minos and Lycurgus [632 d]). As the Athenian says in his ringing address to the new colonists, what god wants is that we should be as like him as possible: and that entails moderation in all things. Failure to do so will bring down inevitable retribution (715 e *ff.*).

It would be a bold man who attempted to give a precise picture of Plato's theology. It must suffice here to say that in Book X, at least, there is a tendency to identify the gods with the souls that move the heavenly bodies (in contrast with the doctrine of the *Republic*, these are now – at least officially – thought of as following constant courses: 897 b *ff.*, 822 a); though this does not prevent Plato from talking about 'the god' in the singular, as in 901 a *ff.* Towards the end of the book, in an imaginary address to a young dissenter, the Athenian proposes a picture of the universe as a single organized entity in which each part is arranged by god 'for the preservation and excellence of the whole' (903 b). 'Every doctor and every skilled craftsman . . . makes the part for the sake of the whole and not the whole for the sake of the part; but you are discontented, because you do not realize that the way things are for you is best for the universe, and for you, in virtue of your common origin' (903 c–d). Finally, god is represented as a draughts-player, moving our souls up and down the scale of existence in accordance with our deserts: the exceptionally virtuous may even escape the cycle of incarnation altogether, and pass into some better place; the exceptionally vicious will

D

suffer the opposite fate (this closely resembles the myth of the *Republic*).

After this, we return to more legislation: the law of property, commercial law, family law, and then a whole collection of miscellaneous regulations. At the end of the work, however, Plato introduces the nocturnal council, which he says will ensure the safety of the constitution and the laws. This I have discussed already; and I shall add only a single point. Earlier, I emphasized the similarities between the studies of the council and those of the philosophers of the *Republic*. This suggested that the knowledge which qualified them to fulfil their functions was drawn from philosophy. But it is also in part *empirical* knowledge; for part of the council is to consist of special observers who have been sent abroad to find out if other constitutions have anything useful to offer (961 a *ff.*; *cf.* 951 a *ff.*). And this agrees very well with Plato's own procedure in the *Laws*: the founding of Magnesia is preceded by just such an empirical survey of the strengths and weaknesses of other constitutions. The grandiose project of the *Republic* has still not been abandoned; but Plato is certainly less optimistic about it.

7 Aristotle's 'Ethics'

Aristotle spent many years with Plato in the Academy, and the *Ethics*[1] and the *Politics* in particular show heavy Platonic influence. Although there are large differences, it is fair to say that Aristotelian ethical theory as a whole is essentially a development of the Platonic. This continuity is of the greatest importance for the understanding of Aristotle's arguments.

Before turning to the *Ethics*, it is worth saying something by way of warning about Aristotle's style. Anyone who comes to the Aristotelian treatises from the Platonic dialogues (and especially those of the middle period) finds himself faced with a quite different kind of writing. The treatises are mostly written in what looks like note-form: they are dense, elliptical, and sometimes disordered. Fortunately, the *Ethics* is one of Aristotle's more expansive works; but even here the reader often has to work hard to follow the direction of the argument. On the other hand, Aristotle's approach is generally much more precise and systematic than Plato's. This is partly a matter of the advantage of a continuous treatise over the dialogue-form (if it is system we want), but partly also of a difference between the men themselves. Plato writes out of a passionate commitment to the betterment of mankind (though he has other moods, too); Aristotle, though he claims the same purpose, is essentially detached and academic. There is occasionally a certain dry wit and elegance about his writing; but for the most part it remains strictly functional.

Happiness (Book I)

Aristotle begins the *Ethics* by arguing that there is a single good towards which all our actions are directed. This is the goal of political science (*politikē*), under which the inquiry of the *Ethics* belongs. Almost everyone agrees in identifying the good with *eudaimoniā*, 'happiness'; but different people give different accounts of what happiness is. And there were some, Aristotle says (i.e. the Platonists), who 'thought that over and above [the] many goods there was some other good existing by itself, which was also the cause of the goodness of all [the others]' (1905 a 26–8). In Chapter 6 he launches into a series of objections to the theory of forms, which show, first, that there can be no such thing as the form of the good; and, second, that even if it does exist, it is of no use for practical purposes. The arguments for the first point chiefly centre around the demonstration that 'good' is an ambiguous term: 'the good', Aristotle concludes at 1096 b 25–6, 'is not some common element that can answer to a single form'. On the second point, he argues that all the sciences (i.e. the practical sciences) in fact aim at some particular good, and leave aside knowledge of *the* good; furthermore, they study even their own particular good in a very specific way – the doctor, for example, does not study health in general, but the health of particular individuals. The upshot is a complete and final rejection of the Platonic vision of ethics as an abstract science of the good. For Aristotle, 'political science' begins with 'what is known to us' (1095 b 3–4), i.e. the facts of experience. At one point, he even suggests that we might do without knowledge of the general altogether: 'the starting-point is the fact; if this were sufficiently apparent, there will be no need of the reason for it' (1095 b 6–7).

As we saw, Plato had himself already begun to move towards a more empirical view of ethics, because of his increasing realization of the complexity of the subject-matter with which it deals. This point is of central importance to Aristotle: so he argues at 1094 b 11 *ff.* that 'it will be enough if our discussion has as much clarity as its subject-matter allows; for we must not look for the same degree of precision in everything we say, any more than we do in all the products of the arts. Fine and just actions, which political science investigates, admit of much variety and fluctuation, so that it seems that they exist only by convention, and not by nature. Good things too give rise to the same kind of fluctuation, because they bring harm to many people; for some have died because of wealth, others because of their courage. So, since we are talking about things of this kind, and beginning from this kind of basis, we must be content to indicate the truth roughly and in outline' (see also 1098 a 26 *ff.*, 1103 b 34 *ff.*). General rules (or laws: the point is the same) are necessarily inadequate just because they are general; for when we have grasped them, we have still to see how to apply them to the particular situation. 'In matters concerning actions there is nothing fixed, any more than there is in matters of health', Aristotle says at 1104 a 3–5: the situation of an action, like the condition of a patient, may always be different, and call for a different prescription.

One highly important general conclusion that is reached in the course of Book I is about the nature of happiness. After some false starts, the argument that finally issues in a definition begins at 1097 b 24. Perhaps, Aristotle says, we can get clearer about what happiness is by asking what the characteristic activity of man is ('characteristic activity' is a translation of the Greek word *ergon*, which literally means 'work', 'what a person (or thing) does'. It was the same word that played a key role in the closely related argument at the end of *Republic* I). This turns out to be a request for something that men do, and nothing else does. Merely being alive is something that is shared in even by plants; a life of perception, too, is something man has in common with horses, oxen, and every other animal. 'There remains, then, an active life of the rational element [i.e. in the soul]. Of this, one part is rational in the sense that it is obedient to reason, one in the sense that it possesses reason in itself, and exercises thought. . . . Now if the characteristic activity of man is activity of soul in accordance with reason, or not without reason, and we say that the characteristic activity of a thing is the same in kind as that of the same thing in good condition . . . the human good turns out to be activity of soul in accordance with virtue; and if there are more virtues than one, in accordance with the best and most perfect. And we must add, in a complete life. For one swallow does not make a spring' (1098 a 3–19).

The key to this argument is provided by a sentence at 1097 b 25–8: 'For just as for the flute-player, the sculptor, and every craftsman, and in general for anyone and anything that has an *ergon* or activity, the good . . . seems to lie in the *ergon*, so it would seem to be for man, if he has an *ergon*'. 'The good' for the craftsman is what he aims at, the purpose of his activity; or, as Aristotle puts it here, it is 'in' his activity (or at any rate in 'what he does'; his purpose may well be something over and above the activity in the proper sense). If man's *ergon* is rational activity, then his good will be 'in' that. But rational activity may be directed towards bad ends; so that one further step is needed. A lyre-player has it as his purpose not merely to play the lyre, but to play the lyre *well*. Similarly, Aristotle seems to argue, the good for man will be not merely to act rationally, but to do it well.

The argument depends heavily on a particular view of human nature. Just as it is part of being a lyre-player to aim to play the lyre well, so, Aristotle suggests, it is part of being a man to aim to live a rational life of the right kind. But this seems, on the face of it, far from plausible. There may be something essentially human about being rational; at any rate, rationality is something that seems to belong to most men. But most men, according to Aristotle, are not virtuous; that is, they do not as a matter of fact direct their rationality towards the right ends. Aristotle's answer will be that our criterion in everything should not be what most people do, but what the good man, the *spoudaios*, does; just as in matters of taste we accept the judgement of the healthy, not the sick (see especially 1113 a 25 *ff.*). The general position that underlies this is at first sight a fairly acceptable one: namely, that in order to discover what a thing is really like, we should inspect a good example of that thing, and not one that is imperfect or damaged in some way. So, for example, a biologist looking into the nature of the catfish (as Aristotle did himself) will select specimens in good condition, and discard those that are diseased or deformed. The difficulty is that whereas there would not be any great disagreement about what a healthy catfish is, or about what a healthy human body is, there might well be disagreement about the other features that are needed to make a good human specimen. Callicles and Thrasymachus, for example, claimed that human excellence was not virtue, but consummate viciousness. Plato attempted to meet the problem; but Aristotle seems scarcely aware of its existence – probably, I think, because he is relying on the Platonic arguments. Earlier, there was a passing reference to the fact that some people believe the fine and the just to exist 'merely by convention, not by nature'; but there is little trace of any reasoned arguments against that view. The issue with which Plato was so passionately engaged now seems quite dead.

I have thus far assumed that the 'virtue' mentioned in the definition is moral virtue. But this is to ignore Aristotle's rider: 'the good for man is activity of soul in accordance with virtue; *and if there are more virtues than one, in accordance with the best and most perfect*'. We look forward here to Book X, where it turns out that the happiest man is the man engaged in scientific contemplation; that is, the man who is active 'in accordance with' a different kind of virtue, or excellence, the 'intellectual virtue' of wisdom. (The man who is active in accordance with moral virtue is said to be second in degree of happiness. In fact, however, this way of putting it is misleading: no one, Aristotle says, is capable of continuous contemplation; thus in the end the two kinds of lives have to be combined.) This is the better, more perfect kind of virtue at whose existence Aristotle hints in Book I; but for the moment it is no more than a hint. His aim, for the present, is to give only a rough sketch of an answer to the problem of happiness; the details are to be filled in later (1098 a 20–2).

The next step is to confirm this outline definition by reference to the things people say about happiness; 'for', Aristotle says, 'all the data harmonize with a correct view; with a false one they are soon out of harmony' (1098 b 11–12). This procedure is a standard part of Aristotle's method. Its justification is given a little further on, at 1098 b 27–9: 'Of these views' (he has just given a list) 'some are old, and have been held by many people, others belong to a few respected men; and it is not reasonable to suppose that either of these should be completely mistaken, but rather that they are right in at least one or even in most points'. Plainly, Aristotle is not proposing that ethical issues are to be decided by popular vote; his conclusions are to be measured not against what anybody and everybody thinks, but against views that are either of respectable antiquity, or else held by respectable men. If Aristotle's method in ethics can be described as 'empirical', it is still an empiricism of a very circumscribed kind.

One final point before I leave the discussion of happiness. At the very end, we find Aristotle using precisely the same language to describe happiness as he used in describing Plato's form of the good: the Platonists, he said, regarded the form as the cause of the goodness of other things (1095 a 26–8); but at 1102 a 2–4 it is happiness that is the 'first principle and cause of goods'. Happiness, the human good, has been defined as activity of some kind in accordance with virtue; and of the other goods, some (e.g. health) are good because they are necessary preconditions of this activity, others (e.g. friends, wealth, political power, 1099 a 33–b 2) are good because they provide its instruments (1099 b 26–8). Thus while Aristotle rejects the theory of forms as such, certain elements of it are preserved – and perhaps also enhanced.

In the last chapter of Book I, Aristotle introduces the general discussion of virtue that begins in Book II. Two reasons are given for discussing this subject: first, that it will help us in our inquiry into happiness; and second, that virtue seems to be the chief business of 'the true statesman'. ('As an illustration of this', Aristotle adds, 'we have the lawgivers of the Cretans and the Spartans.') Aristotle distinguishes two kinds of virtues that are specifically human: the virtues of the appetitive part of the soul, which can be seen either as irrational or as rational (irrational, because it can oppose reason;

rational, because it can obey it); and the virtues of the part that is rational in the proper sense. The first are the 'ethical' virtues, or the virtues of character – liberality, self-control, and the rest; the second are the intellectual virtues, e.g. theoretical wisdom, understanding, practical wisdom. The ethical virtues are discussed in Books II–V (first, generally, in II–III 5, then individually); the intellectual virtues in Book VI. (There is a problem about the relation between Aristotle's account of the soul in this chapter and his treatment of it in the *De anima*, where he rejects Plato's dualistic view in favour of a monistic one. On the face of it, the present account looks remarkably Platonic; but it is probably also compatible with a monistic view. However, the problem is only incidental; as Aristotle himself explicitly says, any more precise account of the soul would be irrelevant to the subject in hand.)

'Ethical' virtue (Books II–V)

The general discussion of ethical virtue begins with a series of arguments designed to establish that virtue of this kind is produced by performing actions of the appropriate kind: that is, that we become just by performing just actions, courageous by performing courageous actions, and so on. Thus, since the aim of the inquiry is not knowledge, simply, but that we should become good, it will be necessary to investigate actions, and discover how they should be performed (1103 b 26–30). After a brief reference to the intellectual factor in moral virtue (discussed in Book VI), and after a further warning about the inevitable *generality* of any conclusions we may reach, Aristotle begins by declaring that the virtues, like health or strength, are destroyed by excess and defect, and are produced, increased and preserved by what is proportionate (*ta summetra*): 'for the man who runs away from everything and fears everything, and fails to stand his ground against anything, becomes cowardly, while the man who fears nothing whatsoever and goes out to meet every-thing becomes rash; similarly, too, the man who indulges in every pleasure and holds back from none becomes licentious, the man who shuns all pleasure . . . becomes what we might call insensitive; thus self-control and courage are destroyed by excess and defect, and are preserved by the mean' (1104 a 20–7). We can judge whether a man possesses a virtue or not by whether he enjoys performing the appropriate actions. 'For ethical virtue is about pleasures and pains; for it is because of pleasure that we perform vicious actions, and because of pain that we abstain from fine ones. Hence we ought all to have been brought up in a particular way from our very childhood, as Plato says, so as to feel pleasure and pain at the right things' (1104 b 8–13). A little later, Aristotle tells us that there are three objects of choice, and three of avoidance: the fine, the beneficial, and the pleasant; and the shameful, the harmful, and the painful. The good man tends to go right about all these things (i.e. by choosing what is fine, which is also what is truly, or 'naturally', beneficial, and what is truly pleasant: the latter point was argued towards the end of Book I [1099 a 7 *ff.*], while the former is entailed by the identification of happiness with virtuous activity); the bad man tends to go wrong about all of them, but especially about pleasure, because the desire for pleasure is particularly deeply ingrained in our natures, and is involved in all matters of choice (1104 b 30 ff.).

In Chapter 4 Aristotle finally rounds off the first part of Book II by explaining the apparent self-contradiction involved in his suggestion that we acquire virtue by doing virtuous things. It might seem that in order to do virtuous things, one must already *be* virtuous; but this, Aristotle says, is not the case, for the virtuous man is not (merely) the one who does certain things, but one who does them in a certain way: he must act with knowledge, he must choose to do what he does, and choose it for its own sake, and 'his action must spring from a firm and unchangeable character' (1105 a 32–3). This last condition provides the starting-point for the central discussion in Book II, in which Aristotle tries to give a general definition of ethical virtue. Ethical virtue, he argues in Chapter 5, is a *hexis*, a fixed state or disposition. But this does not get us very far; what *sort* of *hexis* is it? Aristotle gives his answer in Chapter 6, in terms of the doctrine of the mean. There are, he says, two kinds of mean, or 'middle' (*meson*): the mean as measured with reference to an object in itself; and the mean 'in relation to us' (*pros hēmās*). The first kind is simply the middle point of whatever is being measured, and this, Aristotle adds, is one and the same for all. The second kind, on the other hand, is 'what is neither too much nor too little, and this is not one thing, nor is it the same for all. For example, if ten is many and two is few, six is the mean taken in terms of the thing being measured; for it exceeds and is exceeded by an equal amount; and this is a mean according to arithmetical proportion. But the mean in relation to us is not to be taken in this way; for if ten pounds of food is too much for a particular person to eat, and two pounds is too little, the trainer will not necessarily order six pounds; for this too is perhaps too much for the man who is going to take it, or too little; for it will be too little for Milo [a famous wrestler] and too much for the man who is just beginning to train. Similarly in the case of running and wrestling' (i.e. a diet that is right for the wrestler is wrong for the runner). 'In this way, then, the expert in every field avoids excess and defect, and seeks the mean and chooses it – the mean not of the object but in relation to us. If then every art perfects its product in this way . . . , and if virtue is more exact and better than any art, as nature is too, it will then be something that aims at the mean' (1106 a 31–b 16).

There are problems about the detailed interpretation of this passage; but there seem to be two general points that Aristotle is making. Firstly, the mean 'aimed at' by virtue has to be determined by us, and cannot be read off from an object in the same straight-forward way as can the other kind of mean. Secondly, it will be different in different situations; what is a mean under one set of conditions may not be under another. (The main difficulty concerns the statement that the mean 'in relation to us' is 'not one, nor the same for all'. The contrast with the other mean suggests that this ought to have the sense 'different people measure it in different ways'; for the other mean can only be 'one and the same for all' in the sense that it is the same whoever it is that does the measuring. But that interpretation seems to imply a relativism on Aristotle's part which it would be hard to parallel from elsewhere in the *Ethics*. The mean 'in relation to us' is not *created* by us. It is difficult to determine, as Aristotle stresses at the end of the present book [1109 a 20 *ff*.]; but, as we will see, he still clearly holds that there is *a* mean amount in each situation.) The mean is a mean in 'passions and actions': 'for example, it is possible to be afraid, to be confident, to desire, to be angry, to pity, or in general to feel pleasure and pain both too much and too little, and in both cases not well; but to feel these things at the right time, in relation to the right objects, towards the right people, for the right reason, and in the right way, is both a mean and best, which is characteristic of virtue. Similarly in the case of actions too' (1106 b 18–23).

At 1106 b 36–1107 a 2, Aristotle finally states his general definition of ethical virtue: 'Virtue, then, is a disposition concerned with choice, lying in a mean, that is, a mean in relation to us, one determined by reason,[2] and in the way the man of practical wisdom would determine it'. The 'man of practical wisdom', the *phronimos*, is the same as the *spoudaios*, the good man; for virtue in the full sense, as we discover in Book VI, involves the possession of *phronēsis*, practical wisdom, in addition to the ethical virtues. At first sight, this renders the definition useless; for virtue will be defined by reference to itself. But Aristotle's purpose in mentioning the *phronimos* is, I think, strictly limited: he intends only to indicate that although the mean is 'in relation to us', it is not as determined by anyone; as before, he firmly rejects a morality by popular vote. The standard is set by those who possess virtue, and whose judgement is therefore correct.

In Chapter 7 we are given a preliminary account of the application of the doctrine of the mean to the various different virtues; Chapter 8 provides some more general remarks about the doctrine; and finally, in Chapter 9, Aristotle gives some advice about how we can best hit the mean. This last chapter shows that the doctrine is at any rate partly practical in nature; indeed we would expect this in any case, since the whole inquiry has explicitly been undertaken 'in order that we may become good'. And perhaps, as a general rule of thumb (which is, of course, all that it is intended to be), it does have some practical value, of a fairly unoriginal kind: 'nothing too much, nothing too little'. Otherwise, it at least has point on the descriptive level, in so far as it singles out something about the language we use when we talk about moral issues.

The first five chapters of Book III initially appear to deal with a loose assortment of topics: voluntary and involuntary action; choice and deliberation; and 'wish' (*boulēsis*). But on closer inspection they turn out to form a single continuous argument, whose primary purpose is to establish the extent of our responsibility for our actions. As we saw, Plato still clung to the Socratic tenet that all vice was involuntary; Aristotle now finally rejects it. The discussion as a whole is an example of Aristotle at his best.

He begins from the fact that 'involuntary actions seem to be those that are done either under compulsion or through ignorance' (1109 b 35–1110 a 1). In the first part of Chapter 1, he considers actions that fall within the first category. 'Compulsory actions', he says, 'seem to be those of which the moving cause (*archē*) is outside, being such that the person who is acting or having something done to him contributes nothing to them, e.g. if he were to be carried somewhere by a wind, or by kidnappers' (1110 a 1–4). But there are other cases which are less clear-cut: is it compulsion, for example, when a man does something that is in itself shameful in order to save his parents and children from a violent death, or when a captain throws his cargo overboard in a storm to save his ship? Aristotle finally concludes that these are 'involuntary actions considered in themselves, but now and in return for these benefits voluntary' (1110 b 5). 'But if someone were to say that pleasant and fine actions are done under compulsion, because [the pleasant and the fine] are outside us, and have a compelling power, *all* actions would then be compulsory; for everyone does everything for the sake of these things' (i.e. for the sake of one or the other, or both). 'And those who do things under compulsion and involuntarily are pained by doing them, while those who act because of the pleasant and the fine derive pleasure from what they do; and it is absurd to hold outside agencies responsible, and not oneself for being easily caught by such attractions, and to hold oneself responsible for fine actions, and pleasant things for shameful ones' (1110 b 9–15). This effectively demolishes one of Plato's two explanations of injustice in the *Laws*, according to which a man acts unjustly because he is 'overcome' by pleasure.

Aristotle now turns to the second type of involuntary actions, those done through ignorance. Only if we regret such actions are they involuntary in the full sense. Again, we can exclude actions done under the influence of drink or anger (these too are in a sense done 'without knowledge', but are still culpable). Finally, 'we do not use the term "involuntary" where someone is ignorant about what is in his best interests; for ignorance in a man's choice is not a cause of involuntary action but of vice' (1110 b 30–2). If our goals are wrong, this may be a kind of ignorance, but it is not of the sort that absolves us of responsibility for our actions (here, of course, Aristotle is rejecting Plato's second explanation of injustice – and quite consciously so, as his language suggests). The only kind of ignorance that does absolve us of reponsibility is ignorance about one or more of the material circumstances of our actions: e.g. thinking that the spear we were throwing had a button on it, when it did not; or thinking that we were saving a man by giving him a drink, when in fact we were killing him. Artistotle ends by summarizing his results, and by adding a few parting arguments against the view that acts due to desire or anger are involuntary.

Choice is defined as 'a desire for things in our power following on deliberation' (1113 a 10–11). It is also said to be concerned with the means to ends; while 'wish' is for ends. Chapter 4 deals with a particular problem about 'wish': is its object the good, or only what appears good to the individual? If we take the first alternative, we are faced with saying that the thing wished for by the man who makes the wrong choice is not an object of wish (Socrates and Plato did not shrink from this; but Aristotle has less of a taste for paradox); if we take the second, there will be nothing that is by nature the object of wish, but only what seems good to each particular individual. 'Should we say that what is unqualifiedly and in the true sense the object of wish is the good, but for each individual it is what appears good? And that therefore what is in the true sense the object of wish is so to the *spoudaios,* whereas the object of wish to the vicious man is any chance thing?' (1113 a 23–6).

Aristotle's main target here is the Socratic-Platonic argument that the vicious man cannot wish for his end, and that therefore his actions, which aim at that end, cannot be voluntary. Having now established that he *does* wish for his end, Aristotle can draw his general conclusion: 'If then the end is wished for, and the means to the end are chosen and deliberated about, actions concerned with means will be according to choice and voluntary. And the exercise of the virtues is concerned with means. Therefore virtue too depends on us, and similarly vice too' (Ch. 5, 1113 b 3–7). (The 'end' for the good man is, as we will see, *to kalon,* 'the fine' – he acts 'for the sake of the fine'; so that in his case the end is in fact realized in the action itself.) The remainder of Chapter 5 then reinforces this result, and deftly answers some possible objections.

There follows Aristotle's treatment of the individual virtues, culminating in the long discussion of justice which occupies Book V. I propose to pass over most of this section of the *Ethics,* and to concentrate on a few central passages.

The first of these occurs in the discussion of courage, with which Aristotle begins. The courageous man, he says, will be afraid; but 'he will withstand [what he fears] as he ought and as reason [directs] for the sake of the fine; for this is the goal of virtue. But it is possible to fear [the same things] to a greater and to a lesser degree, and again to fear things that are not terrifying as if they were. . . . So the man who withstands and fears the right things, for the right reason, in the right way, and at the right time . . . is courageous; for the courageous man feels and acts according to the merits of the case and in the way that reason directs in each situation. Now the end of every activity is what is in accordance with the corresponding disposition. Therefore this is true of the courageous man too. But courage is something fine'. (I adopt here the text taken over by Ross in his Oxford translation.) 'Such therefore is his end too; for each thing is defined by its end. Therefore it is for the sake of [the] fine that the courageous man stands firm and does the things that are in accordance with courage' (1115 b 11–24). Dying in order to escape from poverty, love, or something painful, as Aristotle adds a little later, is a mark of cowardice rather than of courage. It is thus a necessary condition of an action's being courageous that it is done 'for the sake of the fine', or in other words because it is right. This enables Aristotle to distinguish true courage from some other types of quality that are called by the same name. First, he distinguishes it from the courage shown by citizens, which he says is most like the first type, 'because it comes about through virtue; for it is due to shame and to desire of something fine [i.e. honour] and avoidance of disgrace, as something shameful' (1116 a 26–9). (If this kind of courage comes about 'because of virtue', it looks at first sight as if it is actually the same as the first kind; but probably Aristotle's point is that the truly courageous man chooses to do what is fine for its own sake, without reference to the acquisition of honour or the avoidance of disgrace.) Secondly, true courage is distinguished from the quality possessed by professional soldiers, which is simply based on practical experience. (This, Aristotle says, was what Socrates was thinking of when he identified courage with knowledge – a remark that has at least some justification as applied to the Platonic Socrates, e.g. in the *Laches*, or in *Protagoras* 349 e *ff*., but which probably does not go to the heart of the position of the historical Socrates.) Finally, there are the kinds of 'courage' that come from a spirited nature; from blind optimism; or from sanguinity based on ignorance.

The point made about the courageous man, that he acts 'for the sake of the fine', is later explicitly said to hold in the case of all the virtues: 'actions in accordance with virtue are fine and for the sake of the fine' (1120 a 23–4). They are also pleasant, and therefore presumably desirable for that reason too – though as Aristotle admits, in the case of courage the element of pleasure tends to be 'obscured by the circumstances' (1117 b 1–2); but it is the first motive that is the crucial one, and the one that Aristotle stresses (see e.g. 1119 b 15–18; 1122 b 6–7; 1126 b 29–30).

After courage come self-control, liberality (which covers not merely giving, but expenditure in general, on the small scale), 'magnificence' (the tasteful display of wealth), and, in IV 3, the untranslatable *megalopsūchiā*, literally 'greatness of soul'. It is worth pausing briefly to look at this 'ornament of the virtues', as Aristotle calls it (1124 a 1–2). As in all cases, he considers not only the virtue itself, but the corresponding vices of excess and defect: the 'great-souled' man is one who is worthy of great things, and thinks that he is; the man who thinks himself worthy of great things when he is not is vain; and the man who thinks himself worthy of less than his due is 'small-souled' (perhaps the best translations of *megalopsūchiā* and *mikropsūchiā* are Ross's 'pride' and 'humility': these at least point up the contrast with the Christian virtues). The 'great things' in question are external rewards, especially honour; and the *megalopsūchos* is worthy of them because he is virtuous. He will be pleased, but only moderately, by great honours bestowed on him by good men; honour conferred by ordinary people and on trivial grounds he will positively despise. He will also be moderate in his attitude towards other external goods, wealth, power and the like, neither being too pleased by getting them nor too pained by not getting them. Still, 'even such things increase men's *megalopsūchiā*, for they are honoured by some [for having them]; but in reality only the good man is worthy of honour; but the man who has both [virtue and external goods] is thought more worthy of honour' (1124 a 23–6). (Aristotle goes on to imply that he endorses the latter point. We found a similar wavering in Plato.) The *megalopsūchos* likes conferring benefits on others, but is ashamed to accept them himself, 'for the one is the mark of a superior, the other of an inferior' (1124 b 10). He will be unable to live with reference to anyone else, except a friend, because this is slavish; nor will he be given to admiration, 'for nothing is great to him' (1125 a 3). He will tend to possess beautiful and useless things rather than useful ones, because this is more a mark of self-sufficiency. His gait will be slow, his voice deep, his tone even; 'for the man who thinks few things important is not likely to be in a hurry, and the man who thinks nothing great will not be excited' (a 14–15). Such is Aristotle's ideal figure. (I have, of course, only given the main lines of his portrait.)

From *megalopsūchiā*, we pass on to a nameless virtue concerned with the proper pursuit of small honours; the mean with respect to anger; friendliness (opposed to obsequiousness and unfriendliness); another nameless virtue, between boastfulness and 'irony' (*eirōneiā*) or self-depreciation; wittiness, between buffoonery and boorishness; and finally 'shame', which 'is more like a feeling than a disposition' (1128 b 11). (Aristotle uses Socrates as an example of 'irony'; he is at least prepared to admit that it is more attractive than boastfulness, because 'ironic' people 'do not seem to speak out of a desire for profit, but in order to avoid pomposity' (1127 b 23–4). Socrates' opponents took a less favourable view of it; for Thrasymachus, for example (*Republic* 337 a), 'irony' is 'deliberate dissimulation'.)

With this, we reach Book V, and the long treatment of *dikaiosūnē*, 'justice'. At the beginning of his discussion, Aristotle distinguishes two senses of the term: a broader sense, in which it is equivalent simply to obedience to the law; and a narrower sense, in which it means fairness in the distribution of good things, and in the correction of wrongs done by one person to another. The first kind of justice ('universal' justice) is for the most part the same as that discussed by Plato in the *Republic*; for in so far as the edicts of law cover all the virtues (1129 b 19–25), justice in this sense will be equivalent to complete virtue – 'not unqualifiedly, but in relation to someone else' (b 26–7). This qualification seems to be added because law itself is essentially concerned with relations between citizens. So at 1130 b 25–6 Aristotle says that 'the things that produce virtue as a whole are those acts prescribed by law which have been laid down from the point of view of education *for the common good*' (*pros to koinon*). 'About the education of the individual as such, which makes a man good without qualification, we must establish later whether this is the business of political science, or of some other science; for it it is perhaps not the same to be a good man and to be a good citizen of any state' (b 26–9). Aristotle's problem here, as we see from the later passage to which he refers (1179 b 20 *ff.*), is that most existing states – Sparta is the honourable exception – are not sufficiently concerned with moral education on the private level; and that therefore it is quite possible to be a good citizen, i.e. to obey the laws of the state, and not be virtuous. (If one lives in such a state, Aristotle suggests, children will have to receive their moral education from their fathers.)

Having distinguished the two kinds of justice, Aristotle goes on to discuss the second kind, 'particular' justice ('universal' justice having in effect been dealt with in the treatment of the other virtues). He concludes that 'just action is a mean between doing injustice and suffering it; for the one is to have too much, the other too little. Justice is a kind of mean, not in the same way as the other virtues, but because it relates to a mean amount; and injustice relates to the extremes. And justice is that in virtue of which the just man is a doer by choice of what is just, and is one who will distribute both between himself and someone else and between others, not in such a way that he gives himself more of what is choiceworthy, and his neighbour less . . . but so as to give what is proportionately equal, and similarly in distributing between others' (1133 b 30–1134 a 6). Plainly, the doctrine of the mean does not fit well in this case; but there is still much in Aristotle's discussion which is of interest.

This is especially true of the part that follows the definition, in which he takes up a series of specific questions about justice. I shall pick out one passage in particular, in which Aristotle makes a distinction between a 'natural' and a 'conventional' element in justice. ' "Citizen" justice', he says, 'is part natural, part conventional' (or, 'established by law', *nomikon*); 'natural, that part of it which has the same force everywhere, and does not exist by virtue of our thinking this or that; and conventional, that part which originally makes no difference whether it is laid down in this way or in another way, but does make a difference once it is laid down, e.g. that a prisoner's ransom should be a mina, or that a goat should be sacrificed and not two sheep . . . , and again all laws that are passed for particular cases, e.g. that sacrifices should be made in honour of Brasidas. . . . Some people think that all justice is of this latter kind, because what is by nature is immovable and has the same force everywhere, as fire burns both here and among the Persians, but they see change in the things that are laid down as just' (1134 b 18–27). This is wrong, Aristotle says; anything that is laid down can be changed, and yet still part of it is by nature, part not. And he adds, blandly, that 'it is clear what sort of thing, among things that can be otherwise too, is by nature, and what is not, but exists by convention and agreement' (b 30–3). There are many different sets of laws, just as there are different types of constitutions; 'and yet there is only one which is by nature the best everywhere' (1135 a 5). One might wish that the problem were so simple. ('Citizen' justice, *to politikon dikaion,* is so called in order to distinguish it from, for instance, justice between master and slave, or between father and children [1134 b 8 *ff.*]: it exists 'between men who are free, and equal either proportionately or arithmetically' [1134 a 27–8].)

The intellectual virtues (Book VI)

The subject of Book VI is the intellectual virtues, but one of these in particular, *phronēsis,* or 'practical wisdom'. We have said earlier, Aristotle begins, that we should choose the mean, and that the mean is 'as right reason directs'; now we must explain this formula, and say what 'right reason' is, and what its standard (*horos*) is. We immediately embark on the first of these questions. The highest part

E

of the soul is now divided into two parts: 'one by which we contemplate those of the things that are whose first principles cannot be otherwise than they are, one by which [we contemplate] things that can [be otherwise than they are]; for with regard to things that are different in kind the part of the soul which answers to each of the two will also be different in kind, if their knowledge comes to them by virtue of a kind of resemblance or kinship to their objects' (1139 a 6–11: the idea is based on a common Greek theory of perception). Aristotle then considers what the virtue or excellence of these two parts will be. In the case of the higher, or 'theoretical', part, proper functioning means grasping the truth; in the case of the 'calculative' part, it is the same, only the truth in question is 'truth in agreement with right desire' (1139 a 30–1). Action, Aristotle emphasizes, depends on the cooperation of reason with desire: 'its origin is choice – that is, the origin in the sense of moving cause, not in the sense of the end for which we act – and of choice, [the origin is] desire and reasoning aimed at some end' (a 31–3). (Strictly, he should have said that choice is the origin of *some* actions; others, namely those of the *akratēs*, the 'incontinent' or weak-willed man, are not chosen in the strict sense.) The virtue of the calculative part is called *phronēsis*; that of the theoretical part is *sophiā*, 'theoretical wisdom'.

In Chapter 3, Aristotle makes a new start. He lists five states 'by virtue of which the soul possesses truth in affirmation or denial': productive skill (*technē*); deductive knowledge (*epistēmē*); *phronēsis* itself; *sophiā*; and 'intuition' (*nous*). Deductive knowledge is about things that cannot be otherwise; when this is combined with *nous*, which is of first principles, it is *sophiā*. *Technē* belongs to the same part of the soul as *phronēsis*, but is different from it in so far as making is different from acting. *Phronēsis* is formally defined, at 1140 b 5–6, as a 'correct rational disposition with respect to action about the things that are good and bad for man'. It functions both at the general level, and at that of the particular: '[it] is not concerned with general truths only, but it must also be familiar with particulars; for it has to do with action, and action is about particulars. . . . So one must have both [kinds of knowledge], or the latter rather than the former' (1141 b 14–22). In other words, *phronēsis* grasps both the general rules of conduct (which will embody the 'ends' of virtuous behaviour), and the right means to observing them. (Since these general rules are apparently 'natural', and unalterable, it would seem that they ought instead to come under *sophiā*. The sharp line between the two kinds of wisdom, as Aristotle has drawn it, is probably impossible to maintain.) But the chief function of *phronēsis* is at the level of means; at the level of ends, it is 'ethical' virtue that is the deciding factor. This is at any rate what Aristotle appears to mean when he says later that 'virtue makes the target right, *phronēsis* the means to it' (1144 a 7–9; similarly at 1145 a 5–6). Whether or not we act for the right ends, as we were told at the beginning of the book, depends on our desiring them; whether or not we achieve them depends on *phronēsis*. (In Chapter 8, political science is said to be closely connected with *phronēsis*: ' [they] are the same disposition, but their essence is not the same' [1141 b 23–4] – presumably because political science is concerned with the state, *phronēsis* with the individual. Like *phronēsis*, political science works both at the general and at the particular level: the first, in that it includes 'the art of legislation' [b 25]; the second, in so far as it is concerned with the day-to-day running of the state. The inquiry of the *Ethics* belongs under political science under the former aspect.)

This provides us with an answer to the first of the two questions which were set at the beginning of the book, about what 'right reason' is. Aristotle's answer to the second question, about what the *horos* or standard of right reason is, is effectively summed up in a sentence at 1143 b 11–14: 'we must pay attention to the undemonstrated sayings and opinions of experienced and older people, or people of practical wisdom, no less than to demonstrations; for experience has given them an eye to see rightly'. As this implies, the quest for a 'standard' of right reason is a mistaken one. (Why then did Aristotle begin it? It is tempting, but probably hopeless, to try to translate *horos* in Chapter 1 not as 'standard' but as 'definition': the translation will fit at 1138 b 34, but not at b 23.) Our betters and elders provide a point of reference of some kind; but in the end it is only experience that can really teach us how to act. This may seem a disappointing answer; but on the other hand it seems a fair description of how we do in fact discover how we ought to behave.

In the last two chapters of Book VI, Aristotle raises some problems about *sophiā* and *phronēsis*. There are two main points that arise. The first is about the relationship between *phronēsis* and ethical virtue: a man cannot be virtuous without *phronēsis*; nor can he be *phronimos* without ethical virtue (1144 b 30–1). 'The disposition [of *phronēsis*] does not come to the eye of the soul without virtue . . . ; for the syllogisms which deal with actions to be done have a starting-point: since the end and the highest good is such and such, whatever it may be (let it be anything we please for the sake of argument); and this is not apparent to anyone unless he is good; for vice is distorting, and causes us to be deceived about the starting-points of action' (1144 a 29–36). 'Since the end is such and such' is an example of the major premise of the so-called 'practical syllogism'; the minor premise would be of the form 'this is such and such'; the conclusion is expressed in action (see especially 1147 a 24–31). In the course of the discussion, Aristotle takes particular care to explain the differences between him and Socrates. Socrates was right to the extent that there is an intellectual element in virtue; he was wrong in thinking that the virtues were merely varieties of *phronēsis*. As I suggested in Chapter 3, this criticism does not do full justice to Socrates' position. On the other hand, Aristotle's own analysis is still considerably superior to Socrates', especially in so far as it admits the existence of *irrationality* as a factor in human behaviour.

The second important point made by Aristotle in these two chapters concerns the relation between *phronēsis* and *sophiā*. *Phronēsis* is something less valuable than *sophiā* (mainly because its subject matter is on a lower level – man, as Aristotle argued in 1140 a 20 *ff.*, is not the best thing in the cosmos); but at the same time it 'provides for its coming into being' (1145 a 8–9). The thought seems to be that *sophiā*, and therefore also the exercise of it, 'contemplation', will be impossible unless life is lived successfully at the practical level. At any rate, it is now quite clear, even before Book X, that Aristotle values moral activity less than he does the activity of contemplation, which studies 'the things whose first principles cannot be otherwise'.

Akrasia and pleasure (Book VII, Book X 1–5)

In Book VII the main topics are *akrasiā*, 'lack of control' (usually translated as 'incontinence', or 'weakness of will'), and pleasure. (There is also for some reason another quite independent treatment of pleasure in the first five chapters of Book X; I shall consider both treatments together.)

Akrasiā is a term for that condition in which we describe ourselves as being 'overcome' by something – chiefly a desire for pleasure, or anger. In Book III, Aristotle argued that acts of *akrasiā* are voluntary; though we may talk of being 'compelled' by desire or anger, responsibility still rests with us. In Book VII, he attempts to give an explanation of how *akrasiā* comes about. The statement of the problems begins as follows: 'One might be puzzled about how some-one acts incontinently (*akrateuetai*) when he judges rightly. Some say that it is impossible to act in this way if one has knowledge; for it would be strange, as Socrates thought, that when knowledge was present, something else could overcome it and drag it about like a slave' (the reference is to Plato, *Protagoras* 352 b–c). 'For Socrates was completely opposed to the view in question, holding that there was no such thing as *akrasiā*; for, he said, no one acts contrary to what is best [for him] while realizing what he is doing, but only through ignorance. Now this statement is plainly at variance with the observed facts, and we must inquire about what happens to the man in this case: if he acts through ignorance, what kind of ignor-ance is it? For it is clear that before he is in the state in question he does not think he ought to act as he does' (1145 b 21–31).

The type of case Aristotle is concerned with is where a man apparently knows, or believes (the difference, we are told in 1146 b 24 *ff.*, is unimportant), that he ought not to do a particular thing, but then proceeds to do it. Having rejected the Socratic solution, Aristotle is left with a problem: for he holds, like Socrates, that action aims at the good; yet here we seem to have a case where a man willingly acts *contrary* to his good. The attempt at a solution begins at 1146 b 31. First, Aristotle offers us two ways in which a man can act 'against his better knowledge': he may possess know-ledge in the sense of having learned something, but not have it to mind (1146 b 31–5); or else he may 'possess' both premises (i.e. both the major, or general, premise of a 'practical syllogism', and the minor, or particular, premise), and yet only have the general premise to mind (b 35 *ff.*). (In the first case, perhaps, he has *neither* premise to mind. On the face of it, these look more like cases of oversight than of *akrasiā*; one would expect *akrasiā* to involve some kind of clash between reason and desire – in which desire 'overcomes' reason. Yet even in the next case, which Aristotle seems to regard as a paradigm case of *akrasiā*, the element of struggle is played down. Perhaps what prevents him from reaching a more realistic analysis is just his unwillingness to give up the basic principle that action is for the [apparent] good. But the whole discussion is extremely difficult, and has been the subject of much dispute.) At 1147 a 10 *ff.*, Aristotle distinguishes another sense in which we may be said to 'possess' knowledge: 'for we see a different way of "possessing but not using" one's knowledge, according to which a man both possesses it, in a sense, and does not possess it, as in the case of the man who is asleep or mad or drunk. But this is how people are when they are under the influence of the passions. . . . So it is clear that we must say that the incontinent are like these. The fact that they say the things that come from knowledge proves nothing; for people who are in these conditions recite proofs and verses of Empedocles'. Next, Aristotle proceeds to explain *akrasiā* 'with reference to the facts of human nature' (Ross's translation of *physikōs*, a 24); up to now he has relied on logical distinctions between various senses of 'knowing'. He seems to envisage the presence of two separate syllogisms, of which only one is properly completed: 'So when the universal opinion is present forbidding us to taste' (i.e. a major premise, apparently of the form 'taste nothing of such and such a kind': my interpretation here closely follows Ross's, in his *Aristotle*, pp. 223–4), 'and the opinion that everything sweet is pleasant, and that this is sweet (and this opinion is active), and desire happens to be present, the one opinion tells us to avoid this, but desire draws us on . . .; so that it turns out that a man *does* in a way act incontinently under the influence of reason and opinion . . .' (a 31–b 1). (The purpose of the last part seems to be to mark a superficial point of resemblance to the Socratic analysis.) The minor premise of the first syllogism ('this is of such and such a kind') is obscured by desire: the *akratēs* 'either does not possess it when under the influence of passion, or possesses it in the sense in which possession meant not knowing but only talking, as the drunkard babbles Empedocles' (b 10–12). Since action depends on the minor premise, in this case knowledge does not lead to action; instead, the second syllogism operates, because it is in accordance with the desire. Finally, Aristotle remarks that all this seems to save Socrates' position, 'for incontinence does not occur in the presence of what seems to be knowledge in the proper sense, nor is it this that is dragged about because of incontinence, but in the presence of perceptual knowledge' (b 15–17). In other words, what is 'dragged about like a slave' is the minor, or particular, premise (in so far as it is rendered inoperative by desire), not the universal major premise. Socrates would scarcely have been impressed. (It should be added that this is not the only kind of *akrasiā* that Aristotle recognizes; later he mentions another type, which occurs when people fail to think at all [1150 b 19 *ff*.]. Perhaps one should connect this type with the first case of 'acting against one's better knowledge', offered at 1146 b 31–5. With this kind of *akrasiā*, plainly, there are not the same problems as with the first.)

The remaining part of Aristotle's long discussion of *akrasiā* is for the most part of relatively minor interest. The same is certainly not true of the two treatments of pleasure; but my comments on them will necessarily be brief. In the first treatment Aristotle considers three views about pleasure: first, that no pleasure is good (i.e. worthy of choice); second, that some are good, but most are bad; and third, that even if all pleasures were good, pleasure still would not be the highest good (both of the latter views are expressed in Plato's *Philebus*, which contains his most important discussion of pleasure; the first view belongs to Speusippus, Plato's successor as head of the Academy). The suggestion that no pleasure is good Aristotle rejects outright: pleasures are activities (or, more fully, unimpeded activities), and are choiceworthy in so far as the activities are. With respect to the third view, he agrees that the highest good is not pleasure *tout court*; rather, it is *a* pleasure: 'perhaps it is . . . necessary, if each disposition has unimpeded activities, that whether the activity of all our dispositions is happiness, or only that of one of them, if it is unimpeded, this must be the thing most worthy of choice; and this is pleasure. So that the highest good will be a pleasure' (1153 b 9–13). (What will 'impede' the activities in question will be, for instance, disease, poverty, or misfortune. 'Those who say that the man on the rack, or the man who falls into great misfortunes is happy, provided that he is good, are talking nonsense, whether they intend to or not' [b 19–21; see also 1096 a 1–2]. The criticism is at least partly aimed at Socrates' paradox about the invulnerability of virtue, which appears also in some parts of Plato.)

The treatment in Book X 1–5 is longer and also more subtle. After another discussion of views held about pleasure, similar to the one in Book VII, Aristotle turns directly to the question about 'what pleasure is, or what sort of thing it is' (1174 a 13). His first step is to attack the classification of pleasure as a movement or process (we saw traces of this view, for example, in the *Republic*, where Plato tended to regard pleasure as a kind of 'filling-up', whether with food or with knowledge). Pleasure, Aristotle says, is something that is complete at any moment, like seeing; a movement or process, on the other hand, takes time, and is complete only when it has reached its goal. Next, he turns to the conditions of pleasure. The pleasure, he says, will remain in the activity 'so long as the thing thought about or perceived is as it should be, and so is the faculty that discriminates or contemplates' (1174 b 33–1175 a 1). More generally, one might perhaps say that pleasure depends on the conditions of the activity being right: the point is similar to the one that Aristotle made in

Book VII, when he insisted that the activity must be unimpeded. In X, however, he is no longer content with saying that pleasure *is* an activity; it is *in* activity; or, more mysteriously, it 'completes the activity . . . as a supervening end, like the bloom of youth in those that are in their prime' (1174 b 31–3). Pleasure is something desirable; therefore, in 'supervening' upon the activity, it makes the activity more desirable, more complete as an end. But once again, just as there are good and bad activities, so there will be good and bad pleasures. 'Now sight is superior in purity to touch, and hearing and smell to taste; so the pleasures, too, are similarly superior, and the pleasures of thought superior to these, and within each of the two kinds some are superior to others' (1175 b 36–1176 a 3). Each kind of animal, Aristotle goes on, has its own proper kind of pleasure, in so far as each has its own proper activity. But in the case of man there is no small variation in the kinds of thing that different individuals find pleasant: the same things that delight some people pain others, and so on. 'But in all such things that which appears to the good man [i.e. to the *spoudaios*] seems to be really so. If it is correct to say this, as it seems to be, and virtue and the good man, in so far as he is good, are the measure of each thing, those also will be pleasures which appear to be pleasures to him, and those things pleasant which he enjoys. If the things that he finds disagreeable appear pleasant to someone, there is nothing surprising in this; for there are many ways in which men become perverted and corrupted; but the things in question are not pleasant, but only to these individuals, and to individuals in this state' (1176 a 15–22). This seems to be a mistake; for it makes little sense to say that things that people actually enjoy are not pleasures. But Aristotle's position is clear: it is that the only real object of the desire for pleasure, which is common to all men and all animals, is the life of excellence. 'Perhaps', he suggests in Book VII (1153 b 31–2), 'people do not [really] pursue [the pleasure] they think they pursue, or the one they would say they were pursuing, but the same one; for everything by nature has an element of the divine.'

Friendship³ (Books VIII–IX)

Aristotle's main justification for discussing friendship is that it is a necessary condition of happiness (and happiness, of course, is the formal subject of the *Ethics*). 'No one', he says at the beginning of Book VIII, 'would choose to live without friends, even though he might have all other good things' (1155 a 5–6). A man will need friends to be the recipients of his beneficence, to safeguard his prosperity, and help him in misfortune; young men need friends to keep them from going wrong, old men need their support; those in their prime of life need them to help in fine actions. Parent by nature feels 'friendship' for offspring, and offspring for parent, both among men and among animals; and so too each individual for others of the same kind, especially among the human race. 'We can see even in our travels how near and dear every man is to every other. And friendship seems to hold together cities too, and lawgivers seem to pay more attention to it than they do to justice; for concord seems to be something like friendship, and they aim at this most of all . . . ; and if men are friends, there is no need for justice, but when they are just, they need friendship in addition' (1155 a 21–7).

Friendship, Aristotle says, seems to imply several things: first, mutuality (1155 b 27–8); second, that one wishes someone good for his own sake (b 28–31); and, third, that each of the parties is aware of the other's goodwill. Three things are declared to be the objects of love: the good, the pleasant, and the useful (though only two of these are loved as ends; the useful is merely what produces something good or pleasant). Accordingly, there are also three types of friendship. These are, firstly, the two 'incidental' kinds of friendship, friendship for the sake of utility, and friendship based on pleasure, in both of which a man is loved not for being what he is, but for the good or pleasure that he provides; thirdly, there is the perfect friendship between virtuous men – perfect because 'they wish each other good in so far as they are virtuous, and they are virtuous in themselves' (1156 b 8–9). This last type corresponds to the first of the three 'objects of love', the good, because the (morally) good friend is good for the good man in an unqualified sense; i.e. he is something 'truly' desirable, or desirable 'by nature', as opposed to the 'useful' friend, who is good for someone only in so far as the latter needs something from him. But friends in the perfect friendship (cases of which, Aristotle admits, are likely to be rare) are also useful and pleasant, so that the two inferior kinds bear a resemblance to this perfect kind; and they are in fact called friendships because of it.

According to Aristotle, only good men love each other for themselves. 'Bad men can be friends with each other for the sake of pleasure and for the sake of utility, and so too can good men with bad, and men who are neither good nor bad with any kind of man whatsoever; but it is clear that only the good can love each other for their own sakes; for the bad do not take delight in each other unless they see some advantage coming to them' (1157 a 16–20). Certainly, given Aristotle's three 'objects of love', one can see how he might reach this result; but it is surely false. We would claim that we love most of our friends for themselves (especially if 'friends' are to include one's family); and most of our friends are not virtuous. The fact is that there are many things that attract us in other people which are not easily classifiable under any of Aristotle's three heads. It may be true, in a very general way, that only what is good or pleasant is desirable; but there are plenty of other things that are lovable.

In Chapters 9–11, Aristotle explores the relationship between friendship and justice. Wherever there is partnership, he says (the word is *koinōniā*: another rendering would be 'community'), there seems to be some notion of justice (or obligation?), and also friendship; and the extent of both corresponds with the extent of the partnership. 'But all partnerships seem to be parts of the partnership of the state; for people come together with a view to some particular advantage, and to provide something that they need in order to live; and it is for the sake of advantage that the partnership of the state, too, seems both to have come into existence in the beginning and to remain in existence' (1160 a 8–12). So Aristotle goes on to give an account of the various different types of constitution, and of the types of friendship and justice that correspond with them. There are, he says, three kinds of constitution, kingship, aristocracy, and 'timocracy'; and three perversions of these, tyranny, oligarchy, and democracy (the difference between the true kinds and the perversions being that in the first those in power govern for the common good, whereas in the second they govern for their own benefit). Each of these constitutions has a parallel in the household: the relation between father and son is like the relation between king and subjects (though Persian fathers are apparently like tyrants); the partnership between husband and wife is aristocratic, that is, when the husband looks after those things that a husband should; when he takes charge of everything, it's more an oligarchy. The parallel to timocracy is provided by the relation between brothers, because they are equal (timocracy being as it were an élite democracy, based on property-holding); democracy occurs in households where everyone is free to do as he pleases. In the case of kingship, the subjects owe the king more than he owes them in love and honour, in so far as he is their benefactor (he cares for them 'like a shepherd for his sheep', 1161 a

13–14); similarly with fathers and sons. In an aristocracy, too, and between husband and wife, the better element is loved more; and this is what is just in this context. In timocracy, on the other hand, and in the relation between brothers, friendship and justice are based on equality. With the perverted constitutions, the element of justice, and therefore of friendship, is small; in the case of tyranny it is virtually non-existent, because there is nothing in common (no 'partnership') between ruler and subjects.

'Every friendship involves partnership, as has been said. But one might separate off the friendship between members of a family and that between comrades. Those of fellow-citizens, fellow-tribesmen, fellow-voyagers, and so on are more like mere friendships of associ-ation' (1161 b 11–14). The friendship between members of a family is discussed in Chapter 12; among other things, Aristotle establishes that the most fundamental relationships are those between parents and children, and between husband and wife. Friendships between 'comrades' (i.e. between people of the same age, who have grown up together) are explained in the course of Book IX. 'The friendly relations we have with our neighbours, and the marks by which friendships are defined, seem to be derived from our relation to ourselves. For they define a friend as someone who wishes and does what is good or what appears to be good for his friend's sake, or who wishes for the continued existence and life of his friend for his sake. . . . Others define him as the man who spends his time with someone else, and chooses the same things, or else the man who shares sorrow and joy with his friend. . . . Now each of these characteristics holds of the good man's relation to himself (and of all other men, in so far as they think of themselves as good; but, as has been said, the measure of each kind of thing seems to be virtue and the good man)' (Ch. 4, 1166 a 1–13). The good man desires the same things with the whole of his soul; he wishes for and does what is good for himself, for his own sake, for 'he does it for the sake of the thinking part in him, which seems to be the man himself' (a 16–17); he wishes for his own continued existence, and especially for the preservation of his reason; he enjoys his own company; and, finally, he always finds the same things pleasant or painful, and is not given to regrets (this is intended to correspond with the last point in a 1–13). 'Therefore, since each of these characteristics belongs to the good man in relation to himself, and he is related to his friend as he is to himself (for the friend is another self), friendship too is thought to be one of these things, and those who possess them to be friends' (a 29–33). (There is a corresponding portrait of the dissension and misery that exist within the vicious man [b 5 *ff*.]. The picture is remarkably Platonic. Platonic, too, is the conclusion: 'if to be in this condition is to be utterly wretched, we must strain all our efforts to avoid viciousness and try to be good' [b 26–8].) As we will see from Chapter 9, the suggestion that the virtuous friend is 'another self' to the good man is meant quite seriously (it *only* holds, of course, in the case of friends who are both good; each is a second self to the other because he is identical to the other in virtue – and therefore, Aristotle seems to assume, identical *tout court*). The idea that anyone, even the good man, can in fact wish other people good for their own sake seems in the final analysis to be unacceptable to Aristotle; and this, I think, is because he tends to assume all human motivation to be fundamentally self-orientated.

This is confirmed by Chapter 8. Aristotle here discusses whether one should love oneself most, or someone else. Two kinds of self-love are distinguished: one which entails always wanting the larger share of material goods or pleasures (self-love in the ordinary sense), and one which entails the same attitude, only towards virtuous actions. In this latter sense, the good man *should* love himself most of all, 'for he will benefit himself by doing things that are fine, and he will help his fellow-men' (1169 a 12–13). The implication of the argument is that fine actions are done at least primarily out of love of self. Benefiting others is important, but it is strictly a by-product of this self-love. So in the following passage Aristotle admits that the good man will do many things for the sake of his friends and his country; but at the same time he suggests that any sacrifice he makes, whether of money, honour, even of life itself, is compensated for by the good which he achieves for himself: 'for he would prefer a short period of intense pleasure to a long one of mild enjoyment, and to live finely for a single year rather than to live out many years in any way you please, and to perform one great and fine action rather than many small ones. And this is perhaps what is achieved by those who die for others; therefore they choose something great and fine for themselves. And they will give up their claim to money if it means that their friends will gain more; for the friend acquires money, while he acquires what is fine; therefore he assigns himself a greater good. And the same will be true in the case of honour and office. . . . It is right, then, that he should be thought to be good, since he chooses what is fine at the cost of everything else' (1169 a 22–32). From a practical point of view, perhaps, this analysis will make no difference; for the good man will still help his friends. But it seems to take a whole dimension away from friendship itself.

The discussion in Chapter 9 shows the same narrowness. Here, Aristotle takes up the objection that the happy man will not need friends, because he already has the good things of life; a friend, so the argument goes, merely provides what one cannot provide through one's own efforts. This is wrong, we are told: the happy man will need friends to be the objects of his beneficence; then too, human beings are by nature social animals. He will not need *useful* friends, or pleasant ones (because his life is pleasant in itself). But on this latter point Aristotle corrects himself. The good man enjoys observing virtuous actions; he also enjoys things that are his own. Now since a friend is another self, the actions of one's friends are (in a sense) one's own; and since it is easier to observe someone else's actions than it is to observe one's own, virtuous friends will therefore help to give the good man the pleasures he enjoys (1169 b 28–1170 a 4). Further, friends will enable his activity to be more continuous. Finally, if existence is something desirable to us, and especially *consciousness* of existence; if the good man's existence is especially desirable to him; and if he is to his friend as he is to himself (i.e. because the friend is a second self); then consciousness of the exist-ence of a virtuous friend will be desirable, 'and this will come about in their living together and sharing in discussion and thought; for this is what living together would seem to mean in the case of man, and not as in the case of cattle, feeding in the same place' (1170 b 11–14).

Happiness: final conclusions (Book X 6–8)

After this, and after the conclusion of the second treatment of pleasure, it comes as little surprise to learn that happiness lies in activity in accordance with the virtue of the 'theoretical' part of the soul (X 7, 1177 a 12 *ff.*). We partake in this activity not in so far as we are men, but in so far as there is something divine in us; a life of this kind will be godlike in relation to mere human existence (1177 b 26–31). 'Each individual, too, would seem to be identical with [the theoretical part], since it is the controlling and better part. So it would be strange, if someone were not to choose his own life, but that of someone else. And what was said before will fit here too: that which is proper to each thing is by nature best and most pleasant for each thing; for man, therefore, what is best and most pleasant is the life according to reason, since man is reason most of all. This life then will also be happiest' (1178 a 2–8). (There is something of a problem about what the nature of the activity in question is: at 1177 a 25–7, Aristotle seems to imply that it is not so much the acquisition of knowledge as meditation on knowledge already gained.)

But, as Aristotle admits in Chapter 8, men are men, not gods. Their happiness will therefore also include those activities that are specifically human, i.e. the activities that are in accordance with moral virtue. These will provide the second constituent of the good life. (External goods will be necessary too – in moderation.) But in the discussion as a whole, the value of moral activity is played down; our real business is with theoretical activity. In this context, it seems almost a matter of regret for Aristotle that man has to be involved in practical life at all.

Postscript: the *Politics*

The *Ethics* ends with the following passage (1181 b 12 *ff.*): 'So since our predecessors have left the subject of legislation unexplored, it is perhaps best that we should look at it more closely ourselves, and in general study the subject of constitutions, in order that our treatment of things human may be completed to the best of our ability. First, then, let us try to establish whether earlier thinkers said anything which has any individual merit; then, on the basis of the collected constitutions,[4] let us try to consider what sorts of things preserve and destroy states, and what sorts of things preserve and destroy each type of constitution, and for what reasons some constitutions are well arranged and some badly. For when we have considered these topics perhaps we might see better both what the best constitution is, and how each is arranged, and what laws and customs they employ. Let us then make a beginning.' The *Ethics*, then, was intended to be followed by a work on politics; and the treatise which we call the *Politics* follows the plan outlined in the present passage sufficiently closely to make it probable that it is the work in question. (Many have held that the *Politics* was not composed as a single work, but was sewn together out of originally independent pieces; but provided that the sewing was done by Aristotle himself, my statement may stand.) As Aristotle makes clear, the new treatise is to supersede all the work done by his predecessors; one of which, of course, is Plato. If the *Laws* existed by the time Aristotle was writing, as it certainly did, his statement that 'our predecessors have left the subject of legislation unexplored' seems harsh, not to say arrogant; but I think that it is at least to some extent justified by the following reference to the collected constitutions. Plato had satisfied himself with suggesting that the citizens of his state would be ready to learn from other states, if their institutions had anything useful to offer; but Aristotle has himself made a systematic study of constitutions, and is perhaps entitled to feel rather better qualified in the subject.

Aristotle's account of his own ideal state is in Books VII and VIII of the *Politics*. The purpose of this state is to provide the conditions that are needed for the exercise of moral and theoretical virtue, and thus for the full realization of human nature. (Existing constitutions, he suggests, do not provide these conditions; their ethos is quite different. But individuals in such states can, presumably, provide them for themselves.) The main condition required for the activities of virtue is leisure; and so the proposal is made for the whole citizen-body to be supported by slave-labour, or by serfs of non-Greek origin. In general, Books VII–VIII do not show Aristotle at his best. But fortunately there is much else in the *Politics*. One of the most interesting parts, paradoxically, is a defence of democracy (III 11). And there are many other discussions of theoretical points which are of lasting value; even some sober political advice, in the context of the treatment of existing constitutions. In the *Politics* as a whole, Aristotle's aim is perhaps as much to describe how things are as to prescribe how they should be. It is fair to say in general that the moralizing element is less dominant in him than it is in Plato.

Chapter notes

1. I.e. the *Nicomachean Ethics*. There are in fact three ethical treatises in the Aristotelian corpus: the *Nicomachean Ethics,* the *Eudemian Ethics,* and the *Magna Moralia*. The last of the three is probably spurious; and the second, the *Eudemian Ethics*, is both less full and less readable than the *Nicomachean*.
2. According to some, this is an illegitimate translation of *hōrismenēi logōi*; but the issue only marginally affects the sense.
3. 'Friendship' is in fact a misleading translation of the Greek word *philiā*: for one's *philoi* can include one's family as well as one's friends, and Aristotle's discussion is in fact about relations with both. But since there is no English equivalent, 'friendship' must serve.

4. The reference is to a large collection of short individual treatments of the constitutions of Greek and non-Greek states made under Aristotle's supervision. One of these treatments, the *Constitution of Athens*, which may have been written by Aristotle himself, has survived.

8 Epicureans and Stoics

The following treatment of Epicurean and Stoic ethics will be brief (my justification was given in the introductory chapter). It will also be highly selective: I shall for the most part restrict myself to a single aspect of the two systems, namely their views on the nature of happiness. My aim will be purely and simply to give a general characterization of the two main directions in which Greek ethical philosophy developed in the centuries immediately following Aristotle.

Whether or not Epicurus was familiar with the writings of Plato and Aristotle, his ethical philosophy appears as a direct challenge to both. For him, happiness lies simply in the achievement of pleasure. 'We say that pleasure is the beginning and end of living the blessed life. For we recognize pleasure as a good which is primary and innate in us; and we begin every act of choice and avoidance from pleasure, and return to it again, using our experience of it as the criterion of every good thing' (*Letter to Menoeceus*, 128–9). No distinction is made between good and bad pleasures; for pleasure is something desirable in itself. And 'the fine' is completely and explicitly rejected as a motive for action: 'I spit upon the fine,' Epicurus is quoted as saying (Athenaeus, 547 a), 'and upon those who pointlessly admire it, when it produces no pleasure.'

But the opposition is by no means as complete as it seems at first sight; for, as the last quotation already begins to imply, the life of pleasure that Epicurus wants to recommend is not the bovine life of sensual indulgence that Plato and Aristotle decry. The crucial point here lies in the special interpretation he puts on the word 'pleasure'. 'Pleasure', in Epicurus' view, consists not only in actively being pleased, but also, and especially, in the sheer absence of pain. Thus, if pleasure is to be maximized, the essential thing is to avoid pain. One means to this will be self-control, which will enable us to avoid the intense pains that accompany excessive physical indulgence; and the other virtues too are found to be useful in a similar way (hence the statement from Athenaeus: 'I spit upon the fine . . . *when it produces no pleasure*'). Epicurus' hedonism is thus a hedonism of a very moderate kind; moderate enough even to allow him to adopt the moralist's pose, as in this passage from the *Letter to Menoeceus*: 'So when we say that pleasure is the end, we do not mean the pleasures of the profligate, and those that lie in getting one's fill, as some ignorant people think, who either disagree with our view or [merely] fail to understand it, but to be free from pain in the body and to be untroubled in the soul' (131).

On the other hand, it is still physical pleasures around which Epicurus' theory revolves. The good life has two main constituents, which were mentioned in the passage last cited: *aponiā*, 'lack of hardship', the absence of physical pain; and *ataraxiā*, 'untroubledness', the absence of the pains of the mind. But the pains of the mind are themselves related to the pleasures and pains of the body; for they are always connected with desires, hopes and fears about our physical well-being. It is in the light of this that we are to take the colourful statement that 'the beginning and root of all good is the pleasure of the belly; even wisdom and [other such?] refined things must be referred to this' (Athenaeus, 546 f). (Even wisdom, because the search for knowledge has its purpose in helping to remove fears about the fate of the body based on false opinions about the gods, about celestial phenomena, and about death.)

Epicurus' ideal, thus stated, seems entirely limited and negative. The highest good, it seems, is to retire from life as far as possible, and satisfy one's basic needs in a quiet and simple way. But there is one rather more positive aspect to the Epicurean way of life. This is the value that is placed on friendship. 'All friendship is choiceworthy for its own sake; but its beginning lies in the need for help' (*Vatican Sayings* 23). It may be that it is choiceworthy because it is pleasant; but it is at any rate a pleasure of a more attractive kind than those we have heard of so far. Epicureans are also said to have held that benefiting others is more pleasant than being benefited by them (H. Usener, *Epicurea*, Leipzig 1887, 544). If this statement is taken at face value, it seems to mean that the pursuit of the maximum pleasure will sometimes involve preferring the interest of others to one's own (Epicurus was himself known for his kindness and gentleness); in which case, it ceases to be a straightforwardly egoistic hedonism. (Aristotle, by contrast, suggested that the 'great-souled' man, the man supreme in virtue, would prefer to benefit others because this would confirm his own superiority.) But this is plainly counter to the main thrust of Epicurean theory.

Epicurus bases himself on the supposed fact that all living things from their birth pursue pleasure and avoid pain. The same point appeared in Aristotle; but Aristotle then went on to emphasize the difference between man and animal, and between grown man and child, with the result that he reached a quite different conception of what is 'natural'. The route chosen by the Stoics[1] is different again, though it has much in common with the one taken by Aristotle. According to their account, the primary impulse of nature is not towards pleasure, but towards self-preservation: 'the assertion made by some, that the first impulse of animals is towards pleasure, they show to be false. For they say that pleasure, if it occurs, is an aftermath, which arises only when Nature by itself has sought out and found the things that suit the constitution of the animal; it is like the sleekness of animals or the thriving of plants' (Diogenes Laertius VII 85–6. The translation of the last few words of this passage, and of the word *epigennēma* ('aftermath') I owe to F. H. Sandbach, *The Stoics*, p. 33). But later on a human being acquires reason. At this point his behaviour ceases to be purely instinctive and begins to be based on rational selection and rejection. His concerns also become wider: he recognizes a natural connection between himself and other people – his family, his fellow-citizens, his fellow-men. The final stage in his development (though it is one that is rarely, if ever, reached) is the acquisition of wisdom and virtue. This stage, like the others, is part of the natural development of a man; for the Stoics (as for Aristotle, and for Plato), wisdom and virtue represent man's proper state, the state that nature destined for him. Thus the goal is to 'live in accordance with nature'.

The Stoics steadfastly refused to call anything good except virtue. Virtue is the sole constituent of happiness; nothing else, from this point of view, is of any importance. On the other hand, virtue itself is found to consist in having the right attitude towards other things, i.e. in choosing the right things, at the right time, and so on; and if virtue was the only thing that had value, there would be no criterion for choice, and hence for right choice, at all. Thus ordinary goods are accorded a certain degree of value, though still held to be 'indifferent' with respect to happiness. (Yet if they do not contribute to happiness, what could this 'value' be?) Health, beauty, wealth and the like are labelled as 'preferred' (*proēgmena*); their opposites are 'unpreferred' (*apoproēgmena*). The first class represents those things that it will normally be appropriate to aim at, the second class those that it will normally be appropriate to reject. Now the man who aims at things of the first kind, and rejects those of the second, will be behaving in a 'natural' way (because his choices will accord with his primary impulse, i.e. the impulse towards self-preservation), but his actions will not necessarily be virtuous actions. In order to count as that, they must fulfil two conditions. Firstly, they must in fact be the actions that are appropriate in the circumstances; for although 'preferred' things are normally to be chosen, and 'unpreferred' things are normally to be avoided, the reverse will sometimes be true. Secondly, the actions must be chosen on the basis of a full understanding of their appropriateness.

This understanding, which is possessed only by the Stoic sage, comes from his insight into nature: that is, both human nature, and nature as it operates in the universe at large. For the Stoics, the world is a single organic whole, of which nature (or reason, or god) is the moving principle. Each individual, in common with every other part of the whole, has a role to play in nature's plan; and since the sage is privy to this plan, he will apparently have infallible knowledge about what it is appropriate for him to do in any given circumstances. It is not surprising, I think, that such wisdom should have come to be thought of as an unattainable ideal. (In a very real sense, the emphasis placed by the Stoics on knowledge and wisdom takes us full circle to Socrates again; and much the same sorts of problem arise in both cases.) But there are two practical applications of this general approach which render it rather less remote and theoretical. Firstly, there is the idea that whatever a man may suffer, however unfortunate he may seem to be, he should bear his lot with equanimity, in the knowledge that nature always works for the best, and that therefore his own suffering somehow advances the well-being of the universe as a whole. (We met with a similar idea in Plato's *Laws*.) Secondly, the Stoics held that in some circumstances it will be appropriate for a man to commit suicide. Exactly what these circumstances would be is unclear, and different views were held on the point; but the many individual Stoics who fell on their swords evidently did not find the theoretical difficulty unresolvable. (I have spoken of the sage as 'choosing' his actions; but it should be added that in Stoicism actions are 'chosen' in a rather special sense. Nature [or providence] is the cause – or at any rate the main cause – of *every* event that happens in the universe; that is, not only of what happens to a man, but also of what he does. As the Stoics themselves put it, our choice is in the end only whether to go along with nature's plan willingly, or be dragged along. This position involves considerable difficulties; not the least of which is that it seems to shift moral responsibility from man directly to god. But these issues fall beyond my present limited brief.)

The two ideas just mentioned above have, of course, become emblematic of Stoicism; and with some justification, to the extent that they express the high moral tone of which it was capable. Unlike the Epicureans, the Stoics took a full part in public life, and especially in politics. Their values, like Plato's, are for the most part summed up in the list of the four cardinal virtues, wisdom, justice, self-control and courage. But there is one important difference from Plato, namely in the value set on human relationships. As I have said, the Stoics held that we have a natural link not only with our family and our fellow-citizens, but even with our fellow-human beings; and the consequence is that it will be natural for us to seek the welfare of others, just as it is natural to seek our own. This is a much wider and grander view than anything we find in Plato (there were traces of the basic idea – about the natural relatedness of human beings – in Aristotle, but little came of it). On the other hand, since happiness is virtue, and virtue consists only in having the right attitude, or making the right choices, not in achieving the goals of our actions, it follows that it will ultimately be a matter of no importance whether we do in fact succeed in promoting the welfare of others (I owe this point to Long, *Hellenistic Philosophy*, pp. 197–8). Yet once again, if that is the case, why should we choose it? Here, perhaps, we come closer to a systematic recognition of altruistic motives than anywhere else in Greek ethics.[2]

Chapter notes

1. I.e. the early Stoics, the main figures being Zeno (of Citium), Cleanthes, and Chrysippus.
2. I repeat that it has not been my aim to give a complete account of Stoic ethics (or of Epicurean ethics). If this were all, it would be difficult to understand the very considerable influence that Stoicism had, particularly at Rome. But I hope at least to have given something of its flavour.

Bibliography

1. Greek Texts

The fragments of the sophists, and the ancient evidence about them, are collected in H. Diels and W. Kranz, *Die Fragmente der Vorsokratiker* (7th ed., Berlin, 1951–4).

The Greek texts of Platonic and Aristotelian works are most easily accessible in the series of Oxford Classical Texts, or in the Loeb Classical Library (the latter has an English translation, of varying quality, facing the text).

For the sources on the Epicureans and the Stoics, see A. A. Long, *Hellenistic Philosophy* (London, 1974).

2. English Translations

The material on the sophists in Diels-Kranz has now been translated in full, under the editorship of Rosamond Kent Sprague, in *The Older Sophists* (Columbia, S.C., 1972).

There are many translations of Plato. That by Benjamin Jowett (Oxford, 1871; 4th ed., rev., 1953) is still probably the most widely used; but there exist good alternatives for all four of the dialogues discussed in this book: the *Gorgias*, translated by W. Hamilton (Harmondsworth, 1971); the *Republic*, translated by G. M. A. Grube (Indianapolis, 1974); the *Statesman*, translated with extensive introduction and notes by J. B. Skemp (London, 1952); and the *Laws*, translated by Trevor J. Saunders (Harmondsworth, 1970).

For Aristotle's *Nicomachean Ethics*, the translation by Sir David Ross, in vol. 9 of the Oxford Translation of Aristotle (1925), is hard to beat.

3. Studies

i) General

P. Huby, *Greek Ethics* (London, 1967), gives a brief sketch of the subject. More penetrating, perhaps, is Alasdair MacIntyre, in the first part of *A Short History of Ethics* (London, 1967).

For a general treatment of Platonic philosophy, see, for example, G. M. A. Grube, *Plato's Thought* (London, 1935), and I. M. Crombie, *Plato, The Midwife's Apprentice* (London, 1964). Grube's book is a wholly traditional account of Plato; Crombie's, on the other hand, is consciously untraditional. It is a drastically abridged version of his *An Examination of Plato's Doctrines,* in two volumes (London, 1962–3). J. E. Raven, in *Plato's Thought in the Making* (Cambridge, 1965) gives a clear and well-written account of the development of Plato's metaphysics. Sir David Ross, *Plato's Theory of Ideas* (Oxford, 1951) is a standard work. W. K. C. Guthrie's *A History of Greek Philosophy* has now reached Plato; vol. 4 (Cambridge, 1975) covers the dialogues of the earlier period.

Probably the best general treatments of Aristotle's philosophy are Sir David Ross, *Aristotle* (5th ed., London, 1949), and D. J. Allan, *The Philosophy of Aristotle* (Oxford, 1952); but see also G. E. R. Lloyd, *Aristotle: The Growth and Structure of his Thought* (Cambridge, 1968), and J. H. Randall, *Aristotle* (New York, 1960).

ii) Early Greek morality

The three most influential books bearing on the subject are E. R. Dodds, *The Greeks and the Irrational* (Berkeley, 1951); A. W. H. Adkins, *Merit and Responsibility* (Oxford, 1960); and H. Lloyd-Jones, *The Justice of Zeus* (Berkeley, 1971). There is a wide divergence between the conclusions of these three books. My own conclusions are different again (though perhaps, despite my initial criticism of him, they are fairly close to those of Dodds), but my very brief account is not written in a contentious spirit; my purpose is not to enter into a scholarly debate, but merely to suggest a broad context for the later treatment of the ethical philosophers – and in particular to justify the suggestion made in the introductory chapter that Socratic-Platonic attitudes are essentially *conservative*. Popular moral attitudes in the fourth century are now fully documented in K. J. Dover, *Greek Popular Morality in the Time of Plato and Aristotle* (Oxford, 1974).

iii) *The sophists*

The most comprehensive treatment of the evidence on the sophists is in W. K. C. Guthrie, *A History of Greek Philosophy*, vol. 3 (Cambridge, 1969), Part I (published separately in paperback form in 1971).

iv) *Socrates*

Guthrie is again comprehensive (vol. 3, Part II, also published separately), although his assessment of Socrates is stronger on the historical than on the philosophical side. *The Philosophy of Socrates: A Collection of Critical Essays*, ed. G. Vlastos (New York, 1971), contains much of value, and includes a select list of books and articles on Socrates.

v) *Platonic ethics*

R. C. Cross and A. D. Woozley, *Plato's Republic: A Philosophical Commentary* (London, 1964), and Skemp's *Plato's Statesman* (see above), are both written with the Greekless reader in mind; not so the standard commentaries on the *Gorgias* and the *Laws*: E. R. Dodds, *Plato's 'Gorgias'* (Oxford, 1959); E. B. England, *The Laws of Plato* (Manchester, 1921). The concerns of the latter are almost exclusively philological; Dodds casts his net rather more widely. J. C. B. Gosling, *Plato* (London, 1973), which centres on Plato's ethics, is demanding but stimulating; similarly Crombie, in the first volume of his *An Examination of Plato's Doctrines, Plato on Man and Society*. Many important articles on Platonic ethics and politics, together with a select bibliography, can be found in *Plato: A Collection of Critical Essays,* ed. G. Vlastos (New York, 1971), vol. 2. See also J. P. A. Gould, *The Development of Plato's Ethics* (Cambridge, 1955).

vi) *Aristotelian ethics*

The commentary on the *Nicomachean Ethics* by H. H. Joachim

(Oxford, 1951) is usable by the Greekless reader, as is W. F. R. Hardie's book *Aristotle's Ethical Theory* (Oxford, 1968), which gives a critical account of Aristotle's arguments, topic by topic. J. L. Ackrill, *Aristotle's Ethics* (London, 1973) gives a selection of texts relevant to Aristotle's ethical philosophy, in translation, with short introduction and notes. The book also has an excellent select bibliography. Volume 2 of *Articles on Aristotle*, ed. J. Barnes, M. Schofield, R. Sorabji (forthcoming), will be on his ethics and politics.

vii) Epicureans and Stoics

In addition to the treatments in Long, *Hellenistic Philosophy*, see J. M. Rist, *Epicurus: An Introduction* (Cambridge, 1972); and F. H. Sandbach, *The Stoics* (London, 1975).

Index locorum

Aristotle
Eudemian Ethics 1216 b 3 *ff.*, *35*
Magna Moralia 1208 b 30, *20*
Metaphysics 987 b 1–2, *30*
  1078 b 27–9, *29*
Nicomachean Ethics 1094 a 1 *ff.*, *99*
  1094 b 11–21, *100*
  1095 a 17 *ff.*, *99–100*
  1095 a 26–8, *103*
  1095 b 31 *ff.*, *14*
  1096 a 1–2, *119*
  1096 a 11 *ff.*, *100*
  1097 b 24 *ff.*, *101–3*
  1098 a 26–33, *100*
  1098 b 9 *ff.*, *103*
  1099 a 7 *ff.*, *105*
  1099 a 33–b 2, *103*
  1099 b 26–8, *103*
  1102 a 2–4, *103*
  1102 a 5 *ff.*, *103–4*
  1103 b 26–30, *104*
  1103 b 31–4, *104*
  1103 b 34 *ff.*, *100*, *104*
  1104 a 3–5, *100–1*
  1104 a 11 *ff.*, *104–5*
  1105 a 17 *ff.*, *105*
  1105 b 19 *ff.*, *105*
  1106 a 14 *ff.*, *105–7*
  1109 a 20 *ff.*, *106*
  1109 b 30 *ff.*, *107–9*
  1110 b 9–15, *116*
  1113 a 25–31, *102*
  1115 b 11 *ff.*, *109–10*
  1119 b 15–18, *110*
  1120 a 23–4, *110*
  1122 b 6–7, *110*
  1123 a 34 *ff.*, *110–11*
  1126 b 29–30, *110*

  1127 b 23–4, *111*
  1128 b 11, *111*
  1129 a 26 *ff.*, *112*
  1133 b 30–1134 a 6, *112–13*
  1134 a 27–8, *113*
  1134 b 8–12, *113*
  1134 b 18 *ff.*, *113*
  1138 b 18 *ff.*, *113–14*
  1138 b 23, *115*
  1138 b 34, *115*
  1139 b 14 *ff.*, *114–15*
  1140 a 20 *ff.*, *116*
  1141 a 9 *ff.*, *22*
  1141 b 23–5, *115*
  1143 b 11–14, *115*
  1143 b 18 *ff.*, *115–16*
  1144 a 7–9, *115*
  1144 b 17 *ff.*, *35*
  1145 a 5–6, *115*
  1145 b 21 *ff.*, *117*
  1146 b 24–31, *117*
  1146 b 31 *ff.*, *117–18*
  1150 b 19–25, *118*
  1152 b 8 *ff.*, *119*
  1153 b 31–2, *120*
  1155 a 5–6, *120–1*
  1155 a 21–7, *121*
  1155 b 17 *ff.*, *121–2*
  1159 b 25 *ff.*, *122–4*
  1161 b 11 *ff.*, *123*
  1166 a 1 *ff.*, *123–4*
  1168 a 28 *ff.*, *124–5*
  1169 b 3 *ff.*, *125*
  1174 a 13 *ff.*, *119–20*
  1177 a 12–18, *102–3*, *125*
  1177 a 25–7, *126*
  1177 b 26–31, *125*
  1178 a 2–8, *125–6*

General index

Page references in italic figures in the general index, are to explicit discussions of, or comments on, the meaning of a given term.